The Light of My Shadows

10 Habits to Shine from the Inside Out

Brencia K. Bienville

10-10-10
Publishing

Publisher
10-10-10 Publishing
Markham, ON   Canada

Printed in Canada and the United States of America

TABLE OF CONTENTS

**Free Bonuses at
www.TheLightofMyShadows.com**

DEDICATION

*To my Most High, Lord and Savior, Jesus Christ—thank you
for always guiding me along the path of light and love.*

*To my most loving and unparalleled mother—you are my
brightest light after my Savior Jesus Christ.*

*To all individuals who have silently but fearlessly walked along
dark paths, guided by the light in their souls, knowing that
the darker the shadow, the brighter the light.*

*To all victims of the COVID-19 pandemic—may the light
of your spirits continue to shine despite the darkness
of this unforeseen shadow.*

*To all Americans, and people all over the globe...may we
continue to fight for racial equality, and just humanity for all.*

FOREWORD

Have you ever felt like you were just down in the dumps struggling to maintain an inner peace? Maybe you have experienced a really traumatic event in your life, which you just can't seem to overcome. Perhaps you have lost someone who was extremely special, and meant the world to you. Possibly, you have had a very unfortunate childhood that left you unsure of your purpose in life. Your self-esteem may be extremely low from an abusive relationship. You may have witnessed a devastating life-changing event that now shapes how you view your environment. Or, maybe you have been carrying a weight on your shoulder for some time, as a result of an indiscretion against you, by someone you trusted.

If any of these situations apply to you, you have made a great investment in yourself with the purchase of *The Light of My Shadows: 10 Habits to Shine from the Inside Out*. Author Brencia Bienville has done an amazing job of carving a path of light and love through her "10 Shine Habits" of personal life experiences, her lessons, her wins, her losses, her ups, her downs, and her life's twists and turns—to ensure you are well-equipped to overcome any dark shadows life may throw your way, and to make certain that you are shining your brightest light, through the toughest of life's experiences.

If anyone knows how to accomplish this, it's Brencia, as she has faced a multitude of dark life moments. Using her faith, her self-esteem, and trial and error lessons learned, Brencia will explore with you many valuable principles she has used to overcome experiences that would have totally defeated the average individual.

Brencia is an inspiration and a motivator of purpose and achievement, and she wholeheartedly believes that you carry a light in your spirit that could help another person out of darkness—if you only tap into your higher power, your why, your purpose, and your core values, to shine from the inside out. *The Light of My Shadows: 10 Habits to Shine from the Inside Out* is definitely the book for you! In fact, Brencia provides "Shine Checks" at the end of each shine habit to guarantee you have an avenue for life application to further cement your "10 Shine Habits!" So, get ready for a humbling journey full of light, lessons, and love as you learn to illuminate your own pathway to triumph! Wow!

Raymond Aaron
New York Times Bestselling Author

INTRODUCTION

As I began to approach my personal illumination of success, having escaped with my life after a nightmarish robbery, alongside a myriad of other unfolding life events, I couldn't help but ponder: "What is it about unique, high-vibration individuals that have been through the rings-of-storms, upsets, disappointments, losses, and challenges?" There are a plethora of distinct figures and game-changers throughout history who have walked along the valley of the shadow of death—a valley in which some of us would have dug a hole, hopped-in, and perhaps even covered ourselves with dirt—which compels me to believe that true game-changers have discovered their whys, and operate in an arena of self-love at all times! Why? Because when you see them, they're radiant, full of joy, all smiles, void of a visible scratch, positive, upbeat, and shining as bright as the rarest diamond, despite their trials. They also move along in life as if they don't have a care in the world. There is just something about them that draws you closer to them, an almost magnetic field of energy that pulls you toward them! They don't seek love because they are love. Perhaps you are on the other end of the light spectrum. Maybe you despise these types of people. Some people may even look down on them, calling them fake, whilst some may wish that they had the type of strength, fire, desire, and resilience that these go-getters possess. On the other hand, you may be that person with true fire and desire, despite the cards you have been dealt, desiring to be a model of success like so many go-getters in our history, such as actress and philanthropist Oprah Winfrey, former President Barack Obama and First Lady Michelle Obama, politician Stacey Abrams, singer Rihanna, producer Tyler Perry, actor Leonardo DiCaprio, rapper and businessman Jay-Z, or actress Charlize Theron . We all have come across, and interacted with, both negative and positive people—low energy and high energy individuals. However, positive energy that's properly used can feed the unveiling of our why, just as it did for the renowned individuals named above. This journey we will go on together will help us to explore how to do just that!

Regardless of where you are in your life right now, my book will undoubtedly take you on a journey to help you to create your own history of success, by allowing your inner light to shine outward. However, I must caution you: Sometimes the subtle but deceptive culprit is that oftentimes we don't know how to get out of our own way! When we fail to get out of our own way, it is easy for us to remain in darkness. So, as you continue to read, it's imperative that you begin to rid yourself of any negative energy that you may have stored up on the inside, and instead begin to create a well-lit path of love and light. If you do this, I promise that it'll bring you from under your shadows, into a journey filled with radiance.

Henceforth, I have amazing news! If you are wondering if you have made a wise decision to invest in my book, congratulations, as you have picked up the right book today! You are in for a vital, eye-opening experience of a lifetime as we explore ten proven and documented *Shine Habits,* which you can adopt to begin to manifest your light, to shine from the inside out. These ten habits will help you to radiate at a high vibration, even in the darkest of times!

Introduction

For some, this journey may be a revelation of what you already know. For others, it may be a difficult but necessary exploration. However, there's one common thing that it'll be for all who travel this path of light and love, and that is the accumulation of knowledge, thoughts, emotions, ideas, and power that will be sure to translate into wisdom for all—especially those who are open to true understanding! Nonetheless, in order to appreciate the true potential in what I'm disclosing, it would be beneficial to not only learn but apply the proven habits that are shared along this journey through the thought-provoking *Shine Checks* at the end of each habit.

More times than not, when we go through life's challenges that cut away at our persona, our esteem, our purpose, or our get-up-and-go, we tend to get upset or angry (which is a natural emotion). We may even become bitter or depressed, and in some cases, some people unfortunately hit rock bottom. Sometimes when we're down, we might consciously and unconsciously impose upon others our negative energy. For that reason, we all have been guilty of projecting our hurts and pains onto others. Unbeknown to us, this is a way in which many try to cope with the reality of a given detriment. Although I did graduate from Spelman College with a Bachelor of Arts degree in psychology, I am not a psychologist. Nevertheless, everything that I will bring you throughout this journey has been petitioned through prayer, experience, trial and error, observance, pain, faith, wisdom, and positive light.

So, with that, my goal with this piece is to share ten habits that will guide you in discovering your inner light, while refueling your tank to give you enough gas to reach the next destination along your journey. The fact that you even picked up this book is a great indication that you want to shine in the most positive way, and I want nothing more than to see you do just that—and trust me, when you reach the finish line of this journey, you will be equipped to light up the world!

So, are you ready to shine from the inside out? Grab your favorite journal, and let's go!

Shine Habit 1
Self-Love Is the Best Love

"She remembered who she was...and the game changed."
– Lalah Deliah

One early Thursday morning, in the summer of 2018, on a solo birthday flight to Pedregal, Mexico, things became crystal clear. Something very profound happened before the flight departed for the friendly blue skies—not as if it was my first-time hearing this, but for some reason I was tuned all the way into what was being said by the flight attendant. She very professionally, energetically, and firmly notified all the passengers on the plane of where to find the life jacket, and not only where to find it, but how to put it on in the event of an emergent situation. Now this is obviously very important, but there was one thing that was ringing super LOUD in my mind on this particular morning, and that one thing was the words, "Be sure to secure your OWN life vest FIRST, before securing the life vest of another person." Have you ever stopped to think why this is extremely important?! It's obvious, right? Because if we don't, we may not make it to assist someone else. While we may be attempting to help another person, we neglect the fact that we have not ensured our own safety—and as a result, we perish.

The interesting fact is that this same philosophy is not so obvious to many of us in this plane ride we call life, and that's okay. Hopefully, after reading this book, you will at the very least have a few nuggets of light, to guide you along the path to self-love as we teach others how to love us by how we love ourselves. All too many times, we ensure everyone else's happiness before our own. We pour love into everything and everyone else first, and we fail to ensure the safety of our own hearts, bodies, minds, and spirits. We focus so much on making sure we are liked and accepted by those who may only cause us pain in the end. We assist others with securing their life vest of love and happiness, and in the process, we end up drowning our own self needs.

The Backbend

Unfortunately, many of us have been that person a time or two; we have bent over backwards and loved those people who may have never fully had our best interest at heart. This could have been a family relationship, a friendship, a romantic relationship, a marriage, or any close relationship. What you may have realized was that the only interest those individuals had in these relationships was to drain you of the love and kindness you have inside of you, because they are lacking love and kindness themselves. Or perhaps these individuals sought to benefit monetary gain, status, a talent you possessed, or just plain misery. Of course, we know misery loves company!

Nonetheless, and more times than not, these one-sided encounters many times end in disappointment, heartbreak, irritability, tears, devastation, trauma, and upset. We are often left trying to understand how a person, to whom we showed nothing but love and loyalty, could hurt us or disappoint us. As hard of a pill as this may be to swallow, WE allowed it to happen! You may ask, "Well, how in the world did I allow someone to disappoint me or upset me? That doesn't make sense." Well, whether we are seeking validation, love, acceptance, or filling a void of a past pain, we are responsible for who and what we allow to get close to our hearts. This may sting, but ultimately we are accountable to ourselves. We have to be accountable for our own shortcomings, acknowledge where we could have made some different decisions, and admit what the reasons were for being drawn to a particular person, or situation; and reasons for being so accommodating.

Many times, we have had early life experiences that have shaped us in such a way that we honestly may not have known any better at the time. Perhaps we were naive to the fact of what was really going on. Could it be that we were searching for something not shown by a father or mother? Could it be that we were extremely sheltered as a child, and are now running like roadrunners in an open playing field? Maybe we put our worth into how another person sees us, because we were never told by anyone that they love us. Maybe we were too afraid or embarrassed to let someone or something go, for fear of loneliness. Perhaps we may have been abandoned or abused. Whatever the case may be, the fact remains that there is an accountability factor that often is not realized until after the relationship or situation has ended, and we allow ourselves that time to reflect upon it, and heal.

I will never forget the day when I finally came to the realization that I had not loved myself the way I know I should have been loving myself, which also became the driving force behind the birth of this book. I became accountable to the part that I played in not loving myself enough, the reasons behind it, and the disappointments and heartaches that I faced as a result. The majority of my years, I always tried to see the good in everyone and in every situation—and I've always tried to avoid conflict at all costs. Call it naive, but that is what I did, and who I was. I wanted to ensure that people close to me were always smiling and happy. I wanted peace, and that was what I often tried to bring to my environment. Chaos just wasn't my cup of tea. I had already experienced hills of chaos at a very early age, and I wanted to avoid it by any means necessary, which caused me to be overly accommodating with people close to me. A few things I have learned is that trust is earned and not given, and no matter how accommodating we are, we will never be able to make everyone happy, and that's okay. I now realize that I was not put on this earth to make anyone happy but my Higher Power (God) and myself. He is the only being that has a heaven or a hell to put me in, so I have learned not to focus on being so accommodating and catering to how others see me, but instead on loving myself—trusting that the right people would be placed in my life by Him.

Failure to Love

I have always been a very strong willed and strong minded individual, and I accomplished pretty much anything that I put my mind to, with the appropriate support, resources, time, and self-motivation. I love myself enough to go after my dreams, and to

4

set goals to be able to accomplish these dreams. However, reciprocal love is something I always longed for—the kind of love that meets you where you are, and matches the type of energy that you give; a love that is long-suffering, unselfish, and unmotivated. You may ask, "Well, why did you long for this type of love?" The answer is that we all long for this type of love, whether we realize it or not. I believe it is a need that was placed inside each of us before we were created. Once I really began to think about this type of love, I truly believed that this longing was placed inside each of us, so that we would long for and go in search of the ONLY love that is present in this fashion. Once found, we would only then recognize that we don't need to be in search of love, because we are love. If He is love, and we are made in His image, then we are love as well. Surprisingly, the only way we would ever recognize this sort of love is to have had an encounter with it before; otherwise, it is trial and error until we truly go to the only ONE who can show us this type of love. Once we experience it, we will not accept anything less—EVER!

On December 25th 2017, Christmas Day, and during a time when I was preparing to attend my eldest, 90-year-old uncle's funeral, I recognized my failure of self-love. My then husband walked out of my family's home, stating he needed to run to his cousin's house and would be right back. I never saw him again. The next day, I traveled to New Orleans for a week to attend my uncle's funeral, and upon returning, my then husband called me and nonchalantly told me that he had filed for divorce. After making sure I heard him correctly by using a listen and repeat back approach before providing him with a dial tone, I called the courthouse to verify that there was indeed a divorce filing under my name, and to verify when the filing had taken place. It was confirmed that there was a filing under my name, and that the filing was done on December 27th 2017, while I was attending my uncle's funeral. Because the papers were actually to be served on that very same day that he called, I was able to be connected to the officer who was to serve the papers when I called the courthouse. I arranged for him to meet me in the parking lot of a Shell gas station near my home.

When I was handed the divorce papers by the officer, from a man whom I trusted to always love and protect me, and whom I loved unconditionally through flaws and all, I knew I had absolutely not loved myself enough to adhere to the initial glaring red flags: of someone that only sought to gain and drain me from anything that would benefit him; of someone who stood before God and 200 wedding guests and proclaimed that I was the air that he breathed, and vowed to do something that was above his level of reason and apparent understanding at the time; and of someone who was verbally, emotionally, and physically abusive— these things, I didn't recall in the marriage vows, nor did I say "I do" to these things. I said *for better or for worse*, but the aforementioned events were definitely not the *worse* that I was thinking I was agreeing to. It didn't take long for the worse to begin. A week after we said "I do," on our honeymoon in the Dominican Republic, a simple disagreement ended in my then husband snatching off his wedding band and throwing it across our honeymoon suite, shattering it into tiny pieces as it was made of a hard metal called tungsten carbide. My heart shattered with it, and I knew this would be a long road ahead if I did not seek God's guidance and footsteps ahead of mine.

Now granted, there is no perfect relationship or marriage. There are ups, downs, and turnarounds, as expected. After my childhood and high school experiences, I was never one to handle disappointments well. I am not talking about minute disappointments of forgetting to take the trash out, or forgetting to put the toilet seat down. I am talking about big disappointments, like cheating on a Sunday immediately after we attended church service, using his hands to express frustration, cancelling planned vacation trips at the last minute, making life-changing decisions that affect two people but with only the consent of one person, and many more.

In an attempt to deal with my hurt, pain, and disappointments during my marriage union, I would verbally express my frustrations of the disappointment—many times in a not-so-peachy or rosy way. I am big on communication. How else would a person know how you are feeling if you don't communicate? I have owned full accountability for the way I chose to verbalize my disappointments and the choice words used to express them. After so many hurts, my mind began to go into survival mode; my verbal expressions of frustrations became very hurtful as I tried to find a way to deal with the pain. One thing I know for certain is that my verbal expressions of disappointments should never have warranted anyone picking up a lamp and throwing it clean through our bedroom wall, leaving a hole as big as a watermelon, missing my head by an inch before I fell to the ground. It should never have warranted anyone cheating, one year into a marriage, on a Sunday after church service, resulting in the young lady reaching out to me to notify me once she realized she was entertaining, and being contacted by a married man, which indicated this was not the first time, but a time of many inappropriate interactions with women that I was not aware of. It should not have warranted being grabbed by my throat and being pinned to the refrigerator. It did not warrant having my jewelry case thrown clean across the bathroom, shattering every piece of jewelry it contained into pieces, leaving another hole in the bathroom wall—nor did it warrant being tackled to the ground in an open parking lot on date night, after a disagreement, leaving a gash in my leg that I hid until it healed.

Even through these events and many more, I tried to stand my ground the best I could, and I still trusted God, and prayed for and loved someone whom I had chosen as my husband. I remained faithful under my covenant through all of its days. My vow was not only to my then husband, but most importantly, it was to God. I was afraid and confused; I was hurt, and I felt alone. I knew in my spirit that these behaviors were not normal, nor were they of God. However, I didn't know what to do. I hid many things from my pastor, my family and my friends. I silently prayed and knew that my God would eventually get the ultimate glory. That was then—but oh, how I thank God for the now! As the saying goes, there is an all- purposeful God that loves us, protects us, and covers us enough to restore EVERYTHING taken from us, so that He may ultimately get the glory! Sometimes experience is the best teacher, and what I learned through this experience is PRICELESS! I have no regrets, as this experience taught me how to love myself more and more—and more and more and more and more! So much so, that during my separation while awaiting divorce, I sought counseling and the help that I needed, to heal from some of the emotional and physical events that had taken place.

Counseling is healing and healthy. It is not to be seen in a negative or unfavorable light. Just as we keep our bodies healthy, we must consider the same for our minds. I used a full 2 years following my separation and divorce to reflect on what went wrong during my union, what went right, and what just didn't go at all. I poured energy and love into myself like I had never done before. I prayed and meditated day in and day out. I started doing the things that I found joy in, like dancing, traveling, working out, spending time with God, and with family and friends that I trusted to have my best interest. The energy I would pour into my marriage to make it work, I began to pour that same energy into myself on a daily basis. It was during that time of self-love that this book, *The Light of My Shadows*, was born. It was what I needed, and it was what helped me get through a time that felt like death in the flesh, on many occasions.

Divorce can create so many feelings inside: loneliness, guilt, anger, sadness, and lost hope. And I allowed myself to feel each one. I did not want to hide what I felt at any time, because I knew it was a part of the healing process; and to truly heal, I needed to go through all of it, while getting the help that I needed to become a better me.

The Revelation

After my divorce was final, I realized some very distinct things: that I had not loved myself enough, that the red flags had been there from earlier on, that I had to take accountability for the way I chose to handle disappointment in my union, that it was okay to seek therapy to heal, that nothing is perfect, that life goes on, that

I had to forgive in order to move forward—and that our God will protect us from anything, and remove anything not in His alignment, if we only open our mouths and ask Him for wisdom, discernment, and a renewed spirit.

Post-divorce was truly that "ah-hah" moment, where the light bulb was on and began to shine bright for me. During the last months of my downward spiraling marriage, I prayed and meditated in the basement of our 3-story home, every morning, for God to remove me from the marriage if it was not in His will, as my spirit was in conflict. I knew that this was not the life God intended for me. I could feel it and sense it, and all the signs were there; I would experience sleep paralysis at times, where I would wake up at night, but I could not move a muscle in my body, or speak. It was as if something was holding me down. However, I continued to work at my marriage, thinking that this was what I vowed to do. Two months after I prayed that prayer, out of the blue, my then husband packed up his car and moved to Cleveland, Ohio—after having told me, with a blank and cold stare while sitting at our kitchen table, only 2 weeks before. A stare that I will never forget, as it seemed as if something of another spirit was staring back at me and through me. This left me breathless and gasping for air, wondering where this would leave me since I couldn't afford to pay for our 3-story, 5-bedroom, 43,000 sq. foot home by myself. My ex had already made a unilateral decision to market our beautiful home, without me even knowing, basically leaving me to either find somewhere else to live or go back home with my mother—which left me facing the lowest point I had ever faced in my life. Basically, he didn't care at that point if I was out on the street; he was moving, and there was nothing I could do about it. I can vividly hear him say, "You can go back to your mother's house, as I am paying for a place to live in Cleveland." Thus, my mother came to help me pack up our 43,000 sq. foot home. My ex-husband did not lift a finger, but instead found it convenient to go play golf and entertain a cigar lounge, while my mother and I packed an entire house by hand, just the 2 of us. I prayed and packed, and packed and prayed.

The day came where my ex left for Ohio, with his car packed, leaving me to re-enter my mother's home and my old bedroom, where I had spent the majority of my young adulthood years. I walked into my old room, looked around, and said, "Lord, I trust you." After 5 months in Ohio, my then husband moved back to Atlanta and filed for divorce two days after Christmas, with the reason, "I thought you were going to file, so I filed first." Go-figure!

Although this was my lowest point in life, it was my highest point, in disguise. I did not fret as I knew this was one of God's many miracles, signs, and wonders that brought me into His alignment. It solidified that He would get me through this difficult time, if I only trusted Him and had enough faith to know that He would never leave my side. My confirmation had come, and I knew exactly where it was coming from—my Father. Basically, my Father filed for divorce, as He knew how worthy I was of His promises, and this was not His promise for me, nor had He put the union together as much as I wanted to believe He did. All of these thoughts became evident during my separation. God said what "I" have joined together, let no man put asunder. So the fact that it was put asunder in the manner in which it was, confirmed that it truly wasn't joined by Him. "Thank you, Daddy; I ignored the signs you placed in my line of vision, but lesson learned!"

I had not secured my own life vest first, leaving me to have to sink or swim as the plane ride of marriage went down in the water. I had ensured my ex-husband's safety above my own. But instead of perishing, I chose to swim when the plane hit the water. I smiled on the outside and cried on the inside as I swam through deep waters, but my spiritual Daddy ignited my inner light source, which shone brightly in my heart. He came and shone His rays of light on me, dried me off, and cast out my shadows, and my inner light has been brightly shining ever since, and I have not experienced any sleep paralysis episodes since 2017.

<u>Fill Your Cup</u>

Self-love is what we all should strive to give ourselves on a daily basis. We must direct that energy that we so proactively invest into pleasing others—whether it is our families, our boyfriends, fiancés, husbands, friends, etc.—into ourselves. Some may think that self-love is a way to become conceited or self-absorbed, but it isn't; it is a way to become aware of who you are, what you deserve, and what you like and dislike, so that others will know how to treat you, by how you treat yourself. How will you be of any value to anyone if you don't pour into yourself first? Until we know how to love ourselves properly, we will continue to attract individuals, and create soul-ties with individuals, who mean us no good, mean us harm, who are self-seeking, or who may just plain waste our time. There are many people like this in the world, and I have met more than enough to know. They stick out like sore thumbs now. Some call them narcissists. Some call them takers. Some call them emotionally unavailable. Some call them energy drainers. I am not into labeling anyone, but whatever you choose to call them, these same individuals are lacking their own self-love, self-worth, and they are seeking what they lack in themselves, inside of you—so be careful. These individuals pretend to be all you need in the beginning, provide you with everything they think you want, and then build you up, to only then "try" to tear you down, and exert control after a level of trust has been established. But the God that I serve, and the self-esteem that I possess, only allowed me to be bent for a second, but not broken, and I am so very thankful for that. In life, we never lose; we only win or we learn. I LEARNED and I WON!

After you have been through a life event that may have left you feeling as if you didn't love yourself enough, you may be wondering where do you even begin to pour into yourself, and water yourself with the self-love that you so deserve. Well, I'm so glad you asked! Now again, I am no expert on self-love; I only know what my experience has directly taught me, and what has worked and not worked for me. Perhaps you are able to use some of my experience with self-love as a start for building something that will ultimately work for you. When I speak to audiences, I often ask the question, "Who can love you like you?" And I always get a resounding, "NO-BOD-Y!" Keith Sweat, you owe me! You are absolutely, 100%, positively correct: NOBODY will ever love you the way you can love yourself—nobody besides God and YOURSELF!

So let's jump right in! Below are a few *shine habits* that I call "The Love Sparkle," which you can adopt to begin to pour into yourself for self-love, and ignite that light inside of you so that it never goes out—even in the darkest of times.

The Love Sparkle

1. Forgive Yourself

Loving yourself starts with acknowledgement. You must acknowledge that you have not loved yourself properly. Recall the specific situation where you lacked self- love, and then in a mirror, say to yourself:

"*(Insert your name),* I love you, and I have let you down. I have not loved you properly. I forgive you for (*insert whatever you are forgiving yourself for*), and from this day forward, I vow to love you with all that I have and all that I am. Knowing that if He is for me, there is no one who can be against me. *(Insert your name)*, you mean that much to me. You are forgiven."

Once you do this, you will have taken the first step to properly pour into yourself, and give yourself the love that you deserve. You have acknowledged that you have not loved yourself, which is a great first step. Repeat this as many times as necessary. Give yourself this affirmation every day when you wake up, until you feel you no longer need to affirm this to yourself. But every now and again, look in the mirror and forgive yourself for anything you feel you have let yourself down on.

Forgiving yourself is so cleansing! It is as if you are lifting a huge burden off of your shoulders. Sometimes when I am sitting in this Atlanta traffic, traveling to and from, I look in my rearview mirror and forgive myself, while reminding myself of who I am. It does not matter where you are. Loving yourself does not have a specific time or location.

Positive affirmations are like Red Bulls for our souls. They energize us and allow us to go on with our day, functioning at our highest vibration—and it doesn't contain any calories! When I first forgave myself after my divorce, I felt as if I could take on the world! My energy and vibrations escalated. I felt motivated, which is the state of mind that you want to be in. You no longer carry the burden of guilt, shame, or embarrassment. You could care less what anyone has to say. You are planting yourself in a fertile ground of self-love that will continue to grow. I would often, and still do, listen to motivational talks and sermons on YouTube while driving to and from work, or other destinations. These habits gave me so much power! So much energy! So, I challenge you to take that first step in forgiving yourself—I promise you will not be disappointed!

2. Involve Yourself in Activities That Bring You Joy

I'm sure there are certain activities that you enjoy, or have enjoyed in the past—activities that will leave a smile on your face and a peaceful essence inside of you that cannot be matched— that give you a feeling of pure euphoria! Whatever those things are, get back to doing those things ASAP! Maybe you enjoy horseback riding, dancing, working out, sewing, or just plain soaking in a tub of warm water with your favorite beverage in hand. Incorporate these activities into your schedule as often as you can, within reason. If you have kids, you may have to schedule this time. If you are married or in a relationship, schedule the time that you need for yourself, even if it is for 30 minutes every other day. Find that something that will allow you to be with yourself, doing something you love, and which makes you feel whole and happy. When you are happy and enjoying yourself, it is contagious. You make other people want to have fun with you. Have you ever realized that when you are laughing, other people also start laughing? Or if you are dancing, other people get up and join you? It's because it is stress-relieving! Remember in high school how everyone wanted to be around the cool guy or girl? Or the popular group? Why do you think that? It's simple! They radiated something fun and carefree! They were always smiling or having a good time, and everybody wanted in on it. The same goes for self-love—once you start to love yourself, watch who you begin to attract, or who will want to be in your presence. Your significant other may even enjoy your company more!

For me, I enjoy full-body massages, followed by a patio hour with a glass of my favorite full-bodied red wine, or Caipirinha (Brasilian drink made with rum). Sometimes it's an evening jog in the park, listening to all the sounds of nature, with the sun's rays shining down on me. It's as if those rays penetrate my very core, and turn the heat up on those beams of inner light already inside me. Sometimes it's taking a solo trip, when I just want to remind myself of the love that radiates inside me, or renew and refresh my inner spirit. It could be a stroll in Barnes & Noble. I love to dance, so whether I am dancing a gig with my professional samba dance troupe, taking a drop-in dance class in the city, or dancing to my favorite ratchet songs in front of a mirror in my home, I find happiness, which is a state of mind that we all have a desire to dwell in, on a consistent basis. I love a great night out with my girlfriends, so that we can just laugh, act silly, and love on one another. Ooh, and trust me, when we get together, we cut all the way up! It goes from 0 to 100 really quick! This is what keeps the heart young and the wrinkles away! Why don't you give it a try for once! It will surely give you a newfound beat in your heart.

3. Meditate and Journal

Journals are like water bottles in my life! They are literally EVERYWHERE! I love them, but I can never seem to use them all. Whether it is morning or night, reflect on your day, an event, an area where you were not your best self, and what things you could do to improve yourself or your situation. If you don't have a journal, your phone is another good option. Every smartphone has a notepad. Use the notepad on your phone to remind yourself of the good qualities about yourself. Every day, think of or write down 5 things you loved about your day, and 5 things about yourself that you did well that day. You will be surprised at what you come up with! Sometimes it's the smallest pieces of our day that bring us the most satisfaction; little things that contribute to big vibrations of energy within us. It could be as simple as letting someone get over in front of you in traffic, or spending an extra 5 minutes in the shower just to feel the warmth of the water on your skin, or remaining silent when you could have totally gone there with a co-worker or check-out clerk in the store. Once I have journaled over the course of a few months, or even a year, I like to go back and read through my journals to see how far I have come. Try journaling or meditating for a week, and see what you come up with! It is the most freeing activity you could engage in.

I am also a lover of candles! So, many nights, before bed, while relaxing, meditating, or journaling, I light a candle. Candles are mood provoking, and they evoke different feelings for everyone, from cleansing, to calming, to romance, to relaxation. For me, candles are a symbol of my inner light that shines ever so bright, even in the darkest of rooms. The scent throw is amazing, just as my inner light is. So, when I am journaling and/or meditating, I often light a candle as a reminder that my light shines from within. If you have special stones that you enjoy, try having the stones present while journaling, to aid in the cleansing of your aura. I particularly love selenite. It is a very angelic and cleansing stone that enhances my vibrations, and allows for a greater connection to my God and to myself.

Practices such as journaling and meditation bring feelings to the forefront, which we may often suppress or hold inside of us. It holds the mirror in front of us and helps us to take a look at ourselves, and helps us to clear away the clouds that sometimes keep our light from shining its brightest. Anytime your light is getting ready to go out, just remember that you have enough fuel inside of you to always create another spark!

4. Treat Yourself

Don't we all love treats! How much more would you love them if they came from you! Treat yourself to a solo dinner at your favorite restaurant, a mani/pedi, a solo getaway to a quiet island, that new house you have been wanting, a new car since you paid the last one off, that book you have been wanting to write, or maybe just some quiet time. Do you...for you...by you...Period. That is perfectly okay to do! If you are on a budget, get dressed really nice and explore a new park with a picnic for one. Go and catch that new movie that just came out, which you have been dying to see. Afterwards, have a cocktail at an intimate bar or lounge, where you can relax. That alone time, where you are treating yourself, is so important! With marriage, kids, work, aging parents, aging dogs, Kegel exercises, and trying to drink enough water, sometimes we neglect to do these very important things for ourselves, causing our inner light to get dimmer and dimmer. Some of you may be saying, "I can't go anywhere by myself; I would feel lonely." Well, let me tell you something; whether you are alone in a movie, a restaurant, or another country by yourself, it sure beats being lonely from a dark shadow looming over you, from an experience that drained you of every ounce of energy you thought you had. So don't let that happen to you! You deserve a TREAT! Get UP...Get OUT...and Get GOING! Self-love for one, coming right up!

5. Recognize Your True Light Source

Everyone has a source from which they gain strength, peace, love, direction, wisdom, and guidance. There are various religions, spiritual connections, habits, and practices that shape who we are and how we behave, and influence our value system. Whatever your spiritual practice, understand the source of which you are pulling from to feed your inner light. I am Christian, so I do believe that Jesus is the Truth, the Way, and the LIGHT! I am made in His image; thus, if He is a source of Light, then so am I. We all have the capacity to radiate an inner light, no matter what faith we carry, because He is the source. Whatever your belief, faith, or source, lean on that as a source of positive influence to direct you—a source that raises your frequency in the most positive way. By doing so, you are providing yourself with the ultimate self-love. For if He lives in you, who can be against you?! No one! His spirit living in you introduces you to your most important "why!"

Let's light a candle, get back to LIGHT and LOVE, and prepare for your next journey of Knowing Your Why!

Shine Check:

Practice the Forgiveness Affirmation in a mirror, forgiving yourself of the heaviest burden you carry. Journal how you feel after this experience. Repeat as many times as necessary for the first few months.

List 3 activities that you enjoy, which you are going to begin to engage in again. How do these activities make you feel?

Consider your light source. In your journal, write down 5 ways in which you pull positive energy from your source.

Notes

Notes

Shine Habit 2

Know Your Why

"She who has a WHY can endure any HOW."

At some point, it's reasonable to conclude that we have all either consciously or unconsciously asked ourselves these vital questions: "Why am I present here on earth?" "What is my sole objective during my tenure here on earth? These are questions I had to wholeheartedly explore as I stepped into my personal journey of greatness. And so will you! So don't you dare close this book! You have made it through Shine Habit 1, and I now have a secret to share with you, which will begin the process of impacting your life for the better! "What's the secret?" you may think to yourself. Well, I thought you would never ask! Simply...to know your why! Knowing your why is a direct reflection of the light that will radiate from your inside out. You will be surprised at what you will start to care less about once you have a clear definition of your why; so many things that used to matter to you, will not matter one bit. You will enter a place of objective resonance, a place of growing peace, and a place in which you will not care if anyone has anything to say about you; a place where the opinions of other people will not matter—unless those opinions are pushing you higher, toward your purpose.

Positive Reinforcement

There is a saying that I love, which states, "When you know better, you do better." This is a statement that has always been very dear to me. Now, this statement requires a little thought, and some common sense. Sometimes we may know better, but do we always do better? No, we do not. There are many factors that may impact why someone may or may not do better when they know better. It could be fear that causes a person to continue to repeat the same behavior, although they know that the behavior they are engaging in is counterproductive to their purpose, their health, or their values. Sometimes it could be low self-esteem, or perhaps someone may not have access to resources that will assist them in doing better, and then some individuals just plain don't want anything better for themselves. It could be a number of factors! So, if it is okay with all of you, I am going to re-word this saying as such: "When you know better, you are more likely to do better, with internal drive, positive perception of self, a great support system, and positive reinforcement." It is my sincere hope that this book serves as that support and positive reinforcement that may very well jump-start the beginning of a lifelong transformation toward living a life full of light and love.

As a young girl growing up in New Orleans, LA, the concept of "know better, do better" was inadvertently instilled in me and my older sister, by our mother, our babysitter (whom was like a grandmother to us...bless her soul), our elementary school principal (Ms. Audrey M. Cox...bless her soul), our immediate family, and our family friends. I am an 80s baby. The 80s, in my humble opinion, was the last decade of kids being raised by the extended village in the same manner as your parents would raise you, without any backlash or commentary from outside influencers. I was raised by a single-parent mother, who was a firm but quiet disciplinarian. She had a way about herself that didn't always require a belt or spanking, although I have received a few of these hard consequences in my years. My mother used positive reinforcement for acceptable behavior, and unfavorable reinforcement for unacceptable behavior most times. And this worked really well for my sister and me! Spankings were few and far between, but would encompass a belt on rare occasions, or a hair brush pop on the top of the head just to remind us every now and then of who the boss was! Typically, the unfavorable reinforcement would entail not being able to go outside to play, not being able to play our Nintendo game, having to stay in our rooms for the afternoon, or removing something very near and dear to us.

The positive and unfavorable reinforcement instilled so many life lessons in me that I still carry with me. The drive and motivation that sprang from the reinforcements were like none other. It taught me that there are always consequences that come with decisions we choose to make. We are in control of whether those consequences will be positive or unfavorable. But we must understand that there will always be a consequence with every decision we make. That's a fact!

The Early Admiration

At an early age, my mind seemed to be on a treadmill. I had many interests as a little girl, and I have many interests now as an adult! Although I enjoyed playing outside with neighborhood friends, going skating, bowling, and to the movies, pretending I had just won the Miss Universe pageant, or playing school inside my mother's 2-story duplex off of Carrollton and Fig Street, I was always very fond of and attracted to parades, pageants, dance, queens, beauty, glitz glam, lights, and all things that sparkle and shine. If you had to ask my mother what I would always say before I left the house, you would hear, "She would always say that she wanted to look like somebody that's going somewhere!" And this always makes me smile when I hear her say this, because I can honestly remember saying this at a very young age.

I was very particular about the clothes I chose to wear, even if just going outside to play. I wanted to stand out. I did not want to blend in with the other kids. I wanted to represent something that was not normal...something rare...something unique. I used to like to carry this little jean purse that my mother bought for me on one of my birthdays. I vividly remember walking through my mother's house and finding different things in the junk drawers to put in my purse, to make it seem as if I had a purse filled with all this "stuff."

I would put loose coins, safety pins, old receipts, a bottle of finger nail polish— whatever I could find to fill up my purse—and I would carry that purse as if it had gold in the bottom of it. I wanted to be like my mother, aunts, and other classy ladies I would see with purses filled with all this "stuff." Of course, it was a big NO NO to go in anyone's purse; it was as if you would get electrocuted if you even touched a grown person's purse! But I would try to use my eyes to peer inside these purses to see what was in there that was so special! So, to me, this seemed like a very important thing—to carry a purse! I wanted to be important as well! So I created my own worth by filling up my purse with things that made me feel important at that age. To this day, I carry big bags filled with "stuff"—it's just that I didn't go into a junk drawer to fill it up at this age! My purse is now filled with the accumulation of day-in and day-out responsibilities that you cannot escape as an adult and a lady: wallet, checkbook, makeup, cell phone, business cards, etc. Ladies, you all know what I'm talking about!

Ever since I was little, being seen as a *somebody* was at the top of my list—not an *anybody*, but a SOMEBODY. Although I may not have had the first clue as to what it meant to be a somebody, I knew I wanted to be in that number. So, because I loved the lights and all things "sparkle and glam" at the time, my mother would take my sister and me, every year, to the Mardi Gras parades. We had a ritual every year! My mother would fry chicken, boil corn on the cob, and fix hamburgers. She would wrap everything in foil paper, put everything in this red cooler, along with National cold drinks (my New Orleans natives know what I'm talking about), and we would go and watch the parades on the neutral ground of Napoleon and St. Charles. I would watch and awe after the dancers, majorettes, and queens that I saw in the Mardi Gras parades, in between yelling, "Throw me something mister," as the floats rolled by. I would aspire to be like these individuals, when at home in the comfort of my bedroom, or in the backyard. My mom even bought me a pair of twirling batons that I still have to this very day! I would practice dancing, twirling, and pretending I was a dancer and majorette in the backyard of our uptown Carrollton home. Pageants were also very attractive to me. I would sit at home at 8 and 9 years old, and pick my top winners in the Miss USA and Miss Universe pageants. It was like going to the movies! I was so excited! It was just something about these ladies that was so attractive and magnetic to me. The manner in which they carried themselves as they walked across the stage, how they articulated their thoughts as they answered their questions during their interviews, and the poise and the class that radiated from them, was just intoxicating to me at the time. And honestly, even after having competed in pageants and marched in parades to date, I still enjoy these types of events, which evoke the same nostalgic feelings inside of me.

Outside of my mom, Phylicia Rashad (better known as Claire Huxtable) was my ideal lady growing up. I was front and center every time *The Cosby Show* would air on weekday television. It was just something about the aura of her on the show, and the aura of my mom in real life. These ladies radiated a quiet confidence, poise, beauty, elegance, and an unbothered demeanor that almost gave off an aura of light from around them. It was a careless confidence, one which said, "I could care less what you think of me; I know who I am and why I am," and thus began my journey. Little did I know that along the way, I would soon realize that behind the glitter and glam...the sparkle and shine...I would experience tears, upsets, disappointments, heartbreaks, and experiences that would seem to almost snatch my very soul from my body. Experiences that would live in me forever, but would play a major role in my "why." Experiences that left me saying to myself, "God, this cannot be the life that you prepared and promised me."

But one thing is for certain, these types of gut-wrenching experiences push us closer and closer to our "why," because it pushes us closer and closer to our Higher Power, and toward our light source. The closer we get to our Higher Power, the more prominent our "why" becomes to us. I'm sure if any of us had to sit down with someone whom we admire as "perfect," they would have a very unique and mud-streaked story behind what you really see. You would be quite surprised to learn of all the dirt and darkness that these individuals had to walk through to find their way to whom they are today. It's all so funny how God will show us a glimpse of His glory, followed by a trial of dark times and low vibrations, only to bring us back full circle so that He may ultimately get the glory. It gives me chills at the very thought of this sort of love, grace, and mercy.

Furthermore, while growing up, I never understood why certain things would happen when they happened, or how they happened. I can still hear the words of my mother, ringing loud in my head, saying, "Baby, just keep on living, and you will soon understand it all; don't be in such a rush to "grow up" or "get older" ...enjoy this time, as it will pass fast"—boy, was she right! I remember wanting to be older than I was—wishing I would hurry up and turn 18 so I could be "older"—so I could go certain places, and be "on my own," so I thought. But as I journeyed down the road of adolescence, to my teenage years, and to a young adult, I picked up nuggets of my "why" along the way. From my adolescent years, I realized that everything worth having doesn't come easy, and thus working hard for things I wanted in life, became my **first** "why." I watched my mom, as a single-parent mother, work overtime, double time, and beyond time, day in and day out, to ensure that my sister and I had things and did not want for anything. She would often go without so that we could have. That is a mother's love. We didn't have a car growing up (my mom didn't drive, and still doesn't), but she would be at all of our school events, extra-curricular functions, games, PTA meetings, etc. If my sister or I forgot that we needed a poster for a class project the next day, she would get out of her bed at 9 o'clock at night sometimes, and walk to the Walgreens on the corner of Carrollton and Earhart, to get one to ensure that we had what we needed to be successful in school. My mother did the best she could with what she had. She would cook us a hot breakfast almost every morning before school, even splitting one single egg between her, my sister, and I, many mornings—imagine that. But we didn't know any different at that time. But now as an adult, I realize all of these actions were love sacrifices that were prompted from the very depth of her soul—the sort of unconditional love that shines so bright, it is almost blinding.

Amongst the Stars

I can vividly remember wanting to win Miss Learning Academy at my private and Christian-based elementary school, The Learning Academy. Every year, one of my favorite mentors and elementary school principal, Ms. Audrey M. Cox, would put on a community-oriented fundraiser, called the Sweetheart Ball (similar to a Cotillion), where the school's student body could raise funds and run for certain titles within the school. She also had a dance program in which dance acts were performed during these balls as the student body was presented to the community. Miss Learning Academy was the second highest and most prestigious title within the school, after Miss Sweetheart, and I had my eyes on it, of course. So, with that in mind, my mother took me to the store, and we bought ingredients to make homemade brownies and candy apples for me to sell at school to fundraise, so that I could compete for the title of Miss Learning Academy. I sold everything! I had pickles, chips, candy, homemade brownies and candy apples—you name it! I was determined! I worked extremely hard. To my disadvantage, I did not win the title of Miss Learning Academy that year, but I did win Miss 4th Grade, Miss 5th Grade, and Miss 6th Grade, three consecutive years in a row! What this lesson did was teach me drive and determination, and the fact that you may not win every time, but whatever you want in life, as long as you strive hard, you can have whatever you want, or come very close to it. One of my favorite quotes is: *"Reach for the moon, for if you fall, you will land amongst the stars,"* by Les Brown. This is exactly what occurred in this situation of me competing for Miss Learning Academy, and this was my **second** "why."

Unconditional Forgiveness

Right before my teenage years, I experienced two very impactful and devastating "whys." My older sister and I witnessed our mom being violently assaulted and raped by my father after they had separated. He broke into our home in New Orleans one night, and cut all the phone lines to the house so that we could not call out; he had used a ladder to break into our home, which was the top floor of a 2-story duplex, in Carrollton. My sister and I were placed in a corner, facing the wall, while my dad violently assaulted and raped my mom right before us—all we could hear were shrills of cries and screams. This was a very traumatic experience, and as a 12-year-old child, I was faced with having to potentially testify against my own father, who ended up going to prison for the crime he had committed. This incident was one of many that we witnessed growing up. On another occasion when I was 5 years old, we witnessed my dad boil a gumbo pot of water until it was scalding hot. As my mother and I tried to run out of the house, he threw the scalding pot of water on my mother, leaving her in the hospital with 3rd and 4th degree burns, as well as a broken leg. Tragically enough, I was standing near her, but managed to escape the scalding water. As horrific as these incidents were for us, I had to find it in my heart to ultimately forgive my dad in order to be able to move on with my life. Granted, this forgiveness did not come until later in my adult life; however, I knew it was what God would have me do, as hard as it was. I did not want to subject myself to a burden that could potentially hinder me from establishing relationships with men, nor did I care to have a darkness over me that would only provide an avenue for Satan to work.

So yes, I forgave my dad, and I asked my God above to remove any ounce of pain, grief, bondage, or reflection of these incidents. Despite the horrific crimes that we witnessed, I love my dad, because if not for him, there would be no me. I have purpose despite his actions. In order for me not to have a shadow over me, I had to forgive him and love him with the type of love that is uncompromising. I dare not judge him, as this is not my place to do so, although I did for a very long time. As I became more mature as a young adult, I realized that I needed to love my dad the same way my Lord loves me; regardless of my shortcomings, He is always there to pick me up, dust me off, and love on me. I wanted to display that type of love for my dad. Sometimes we are quick to judge, but I have learned that sometimes if you treat people with love, the light that you give off may start to brighten the shadow the other person may be walking in; thus, this is my **third** "why" that I picked up along my journey.

<u>Size of a Mustard Seed</u>

Months after the traumatic incident with my dad, my family experienced an unexpected relocation from the only place we ever knew as home, to a state where we did not know anyone, period. This state was Georgia. Little could I fathom, this move would be one of the best blessings that God could have bestowed upon my family at that time. One thing is for sure, God is always 10 steps ahead of us with His plan. As devastating and traumatic as both of those experiences were, He had never left us or forsaken my family. He blessed us by removing us from a situation that could have ultimately killed us, and placed us in a state of peace (no pun intended). We moved to Georgia in the summer of 1993. I was going into 8th grade, which was a part of the high school, and did not know a single person. I think I almost went into a bit of a depression; so much so that my mother thought that she would have to send me back to New Orleans to live with family until I finished high school. Back when kids still wrote letters and had pen pals, I would write letters to my friends in New Orleans, and talk to them on the "house phone" when I could. There was no social media to keep up with anyone, nor Facetime to experience a real live conversation. So this pretty much continued throughout the entire summer until school began in the fall.

I remember the day of registration at my new school—my first time I would be going to high school. Although my sister was 3 years older, I would at least have her with me my first year in high school. We walked into the gymnasium, and it was filled with all sorts of students, tables, teachers, etc. I stood back and watched all of what was transpiring in front of me. I think my mother knew that I would not go up to any of those tables and speak to anyone, so she took it upon herself to go up to the cheerleading table, where the current cheerleaders were gathered and talking amongst themselves and to other students stopping by.

I had cheered at my catholic middle school prior to relocating to Atlanta, so my mother thought that perhaps cheerleading would interest me. After speaking with the girls briefly, she motioned me over to the table. I slowly walked over; my mother introduced me to the group, and they began to talk to me and ask me questions. They were extremely nice, to my surprise! So they told me a bit about the cheerleading program and offered me an audition form to complete. I completed the form and gave it back...weeks later, I found myself at cheerleading auditions! By then, I had made a few friends in my classes, and was starting to feel a bit of a relief. I still missed my friends in New Orleans, but I was starting to enjoy my new school. I was actually excited for auditions!

I did my best and my best paid off, as I saw my name under the new Junior Varsity cheerleading squad for the football season! I was ecstatic! This was the beginning of what would turn out to be a wonderful high school experience at Chamblee High School. I soon started to make even more friends. Everyone knew who I was at this point, as cheerleaders are involved in many events during the year. I was even voted and won the title of Miss 8th Grade that year! So, things were on the up and up, and I was starting to feel really good about the move at this point. So, my **fourth** "why" was to have faith the size of a mustard seed, and always trust that God has our best interest at heart, regardless of what we think.

<u>Sharing is Caring</u>

Over the course of my high school journey, I made some really good friends, joined numerous social and scholastic clubs, participated in pageants, and even won Prom Queen my senior year, and Miss Black Teen of Atlanta 1998, my senior year— none of which I would have ever imagined prior to me moving to Atlanta! As I journeyed through high school, I began to ponder what I wanted to be as an adult. I knew that college would be the next phase for me after high school, but I wanted to at least have an idea of what my interests were for a career.

While still living in New Orleans, my sister was diagnosed with Type 1 juvenile diabetes, at 12 years old. So being 3 years younger than she was, I would administer insulin shots to her when I was only 9 years old. At an early age, I needed to understand what her medical condition was, in the event she ever experienced an emergency, which she did on a few occasions. On one occasion, on a girls' trip to Los Angeles in the early 2000s, my sister went to bed without eating, although she had given herself an insulin dose. With diabetes, your body is incapable of producing insulin on its own (which is produced by the pancreas, and helps control blood glucose levels by signaling the liver, muscle, and fat to take in sugar from the blood), so insulin shots must be administered. Because she did not eat, but had given her body the insulin shot, her blood glucose dropped dangerously low.

As we all arose the next morning to prepare to go on *The Price Is Right* game show, my sister did not move. I thought perhaps she was just getting a few extra minutes of sleep, until I called her name, and she was not moving but was uttering gibberish. So in a panic, we called 911, and tried to find juice and candy to give her. By the time the paramedics arrived, her blood sugar was critically low. They treated her from the hotel room with a bolus of sugar, and monitored her until her blood glucose levels stabilized. Needless to say, we did not make it onto *The Price Is Right*, but most importantly, my sister was still with us; thus, my desire and passion to care for other people was inspired at an early age, when my sister was diagnosed with diabetes. I knew that I wanted to go into healthcare. I didn't know exactly what it would be, but I knew it was in me and a part of me. I enrolled in Advanced Placement science classes in high school, and began to prepare myself as best I could for a potential career in healthcare. So my **fifth** "why" evolved into caring for and lending a helping hand to those that are less fortunate than I am. What did this fifth "why" transpire to, later in life? Yep, you guessed it: becoming a registered nurse, where caring for people and teaching patients became a real passion of mine.

A Good Report

When I moved to Atlanta, I secured my first job, working as a bagger at the nearby Kroger grocery store, at 14 years old. That lasted all of 1 month, when I was asked to go outside and gather grocery baskets from the parking lot, in 97 degree Atlanta heat! I didn't know what it meant when I would hear people say "HOTLanta," but it didn't take me long to realize that it was a blaze of heat that made you feel as if someone had lit a match on your skin. I couldn't do it. So I left Kroger, and I went to work at Wendy's as a cashier, around the corner from my mother's apartment complex.

I was really starting to settle in at my new job, when one night, while at the front register, two men walked in and proceeded to order food. As I eagerly looked up from taking the order, all I felt was a gun to my head as one of the men hopped over the counter, and the other man ran through the side door to the back kitchen. I hit the floor and saw my entire life flash before me. I don't even remember getting the money out of the register, but I managed to compose myself enough to try to comply with the eerie request of the robber, who had hopped over the counter and still had the gun against me. It all happened so extremely fast, and they were gone in a flash as I lay on the floor with a tear-soaked face. This event was a true testimony that there clearly was a bigger "why" for me, and it was just not my time to go yet. So the question of what is my purpose, became even more prominent in my head after that night.

I began to wonder, if my life had been taken that night, how would people have remembered me? What would they have said about me? So, at that point, I began living each day as if it was truly my last, leaving no stone unturned. I did not want to have any regrets from that point forward. I began to take advantage of each opportunity that would allow me to expand myself and inspire the next person at the same time. At the end of the day, I wanted my report to read: "Job well done, my good and faithful daughter." You guessed it! Yep, my "why" number **six**.

<u>No Record of Wrong</u>

Unfortunately, while a senior in high school, I had to face one of the most difficult decisions my young mind could bear, right before my senior graduation. I found out I was pregnant with twins, by the only high school boyfriend I had ever known. I was scared, embarrassed, and didn't know what to do. I had been accepted to Spelman College, and was preparing to begin as a freshman in the fall of that year. Afraid to tell my mother and disappoint her after all of her efforts, I made a decision that haunted me for a very long time. I ended the pregnancy without telling my mother, or anyone besides my boyfriend at the time.

I could not bear the guilt of what I had done, so I eventually told her the mistake I had made, and what I had done. I will never forget the look on her face as she stared at me in silence. It is a face that is drawn in my mind forever. This hurt me deeply as I never wanted to do anything to hurt her after all of her sacrifices, and all she had endured. But because of who she is and the unconditional love she had and still has for me as her child, she did not scold me; she expressed her disappointment, and proceeded to ensure that I was okay. I prayed and asked God for the forgiveness that I knew only He could grant; and although we know that when we pray and ask for forgiveness, it is done in His name, my young mind would not let me rest for many years. I would get emotional if I thought about it, or if I thought about who those twins would have grown up to become in this world. To this very day, I love them both with all my heart and soul, and I always will.

While in college, I decided I could not bear the burden of guilt anymore, and I decided to pray a prayer one more time, with the most humbled and convicted spirit. I lay before God and soaked my entire pillow case, down to the actual cotton in the pillow. What He showed me that night was that He is a just and forgiving God who keeps no record of wrong-doing once we are forgiven. He showed me that there are consequences to every decision we make in life, and we have to be ready to face the consequence as much as the decision. The shadow that had hung over me, prior to my prayer, was dark and heavy, but I felt a huge release and lift that night, and I knew it was done in His mighty name. I saw a glimmer of light, and I knew all would be well. I learned a very valuable lesson that night: to ALWAYS trust God in all of my doings, whether good or bad, and to never lean unto my own understanding; to trust in Him, and He will surely direct my path—and He did.

Fire to Refinement

At my senior high school graduation, I was humbled in the most major way, as the principal at the time, Dr. Martha Reithcraft, awarded me with the Principal's Cup! I was certainly not expecting this. As I walked up to accept the honor, with tears in my eyes and a tremble in my heart, I reflected on the beginning of my journey, from New Orleans to Atlanta, and how unaccepting I was at first of the relocation to another state. All of the dark events that had occurred in my life up to that point, played in mind. I felt I was truly undeserving of such an honor. But over the course of 4 years in high school, God truly showed me that it is not what we want, but what is in His will for us—and no matter how unworthy we may feel at times, we are always worthy in His eyes, and what He has for us, no one can take that away. It is the unmerited favor and love that He shows us—called grace. One thing is for sure, He may not always give us what we want, but he will always give us what we need, in His time, and for that I am forever thankful.

There is something about when you know your "why," and the peace that comes over you. You are not frantically searching for a reason to exist. We all have been guilty of this at some point or another. We look at other people's lives and compare ourselves to them. We think that everyone else has it figured out. In all truth, those same people are looking at you because they think you have it figured out, not realizing that we each have to go through the fire of refinement. If each of us would focus on trying to figure out our OWN "why," we would be too busy to pay attention to whether the next person has it together or not. We each have our "why" hidden inside of us. We only need to quieten our spirits, find the purpose in pain, and allow the lesson to be our light.

One thing about allowing our light to shine from the inside out, is that we are aware of our "why." We are aware of our purpose. We must have faith in that purpose, and we must make that purpose an action. He never promised us that this life would be easy, but that it would be worth it, and it would be unique to us in our very special way.

Let's explore exactly what makes us so extremely unique, in our next *Shine Habit*! You owe it to yourself to be your own kind of beautiful!

Shine Check:

In this shine habit, we have learned that in order to radiate from the inside out, we must:

- Understand that a painful experience often leads to a purposeful experience.
- Try to live every day in a way that will create admiration and inspiration for the next person.
- Shoot for the moon in all we do; if we miss, the stars are right there to catch us.
- Show unconditional forgiveness to someone, regardless if we think they deserve it or not.
- Know that faith is trusting that our Higher Power has our best interest.
- Always care for and assist those people less fortunate than ourselves.
- Live to achieve a "Job Well Done" report.
- Know that whether we believe we are deserving or not, we will always be deserving in the eyes of our Creator.
- Know that regardless of what misfortunes have happened to us along our journey, it is the fire that refines us to receive all that is in store for us.

Notes

Shine Habit 3

Be Uniquely You

"You will never influence the world by being just like it."

Now let's be honest, we have all looked at another person's family, career, car, home, life, or even intellect, and wanted to be or have what someone else has, or do what someone else is doing—or wondered how their life is just that perfect! We all have done this a time or two or three or four! I know I have! Growing up in New Orleans, my family didn't own a car, and I wanted us to have a car so bad! We rode the RTA (Rapid Transit Authority) everywhere, better known as the city bus, or we hopped in United taxis. I remember wishing we could have a car just like some of my friends' parents. But the reason my family never had a car is because my mother did not drive; she never has. My sister was in college when she purchased her first car, and I was in my junior year of college when my mother bought our very first car for me to drive.

Nonetheless, there is just something about wanting, almost to an obsession at times, what someone else has, or to do what someone else is doing. Why do we do this to ourselves?! Is it because we think our lives will be easier with what someone else has? Is it because we admire the person or thing for what they have? Or perhaps there is something deep inside of us that we need to come to grips with? Why do we feel that everyone, besides our own self, has it all figured out? None of us have this thing called life down to a science, whether we believe we do or not.

We are each on an individual journey, a constant progression toward the finish line. We may go fast, go slow, hydroplane, spin out, or even run out of gas along the way. This is what makes each of us so uniquely different. No two people have the EXACT same story, same journey, or same DNA. How boring would life be if this were so?! Because each of us are made in His image, but uniquely different, it brings beauty to this earthly realm. Embracing the total uniqueness of yourself is like a wall dimmer—the more we truly embrace our uniqueness, the brighter our inner light will shine as we continue to push onwards and upwards.

Keeping Up

I have never been a big fan of fads and "keeping up with the Joneses." For what?! Why try to keep up when we were born to stand out?! It's a simple question that many of us probably can't answer with any amount of logic. But surely there are underlying reasons that may or may not readily come to mind when trying to answer these questions. When we "keep up with the Joneses," we subconsciously mask our uniqueness. Fundamentally, the obvious holds true of adolescents. Most adolescents are intrigued with "keeping up" with their peers. Growing up in the 80s and 90s, polo shirts, Gibeaux jeans, Eastlands, Esprit, and medallion earrings were the thing in New Orleans! You were seen as all that and several bags of Zapps crawfish flavored potato chips if you had this "fit" on! So, what did I ask for one Christmas on my wish list, outside of the African Holiday Barbie?! You guessed it! A striped, multi-colored polo shirt, Gibeaux jeans, and a pair of purple Eastlands! You could not tell me a single thing! I knew I was the best thing smoking! What I didn't realize was how much more of a tom boy it made me look, and how I now looked like everyone else—there was nothing unique about me anymore. I looked like everyone else that was trying to fit in. It wasn't until I moved to Atlanta, when I was in high school, that I realized a polo shirt, Gibeaux jeans, and medallion earrings meant nothing to my friends. I realized that I didn't like how I looked anymore, because it wasn't truly who I was. I was all girl on the inside, but me trying to fit in and "keep up" with my peers, in elementary and middle school, masked my inner girly girl. I realized that I liked dresses, sandals, and tank tops. My sister and I didn't really get to pick our clothes during the school year. Sometimes we did, especially during school shopping time, but for the most part, my mother would go to Macy's or Dillard's when she got off work in the evenings, and buy some clothing items and hang them on our bedroom door. We never said we didn't like it. We were extremely appreciative! My mother has good taste, but even if she did not, we did not complain about anything that she brought to us, which she had spent her hard earned money on.

The Relevance of Practicality

Now let's not get this totally confused. Is it okay to aspire to have nice things? Absolutely, it is! But not because someone else has it, or because we want to "appear" to have it going on, and not to succumb to peer pressure or some sort of adult popularity contest or the like. We want to strive to "have it going on" because we are just that relevant by what our spirit radiates, how we treat others, what we are doing for the community, and for the paths we are paving for generations behind us—not because we have the newest Chanel bag, the hottest car, or a million fake followers on social media. Having it "going on" should come from the inside out, not the outside in. It should be an unspoken magnet of attraction by others that is not built on material gains, but instead built on the gains of a character that is seen and not heard. Being seen and not heard has always been a motto of mine, and striving to be practical in all I do is another.

My mother always taught me to always be practical in all that I do. Practical is not carrying a Gucci or Chanel purse without enough money on your paystub, in the bank, or in your 401K that matches or exceeds the cost of your bag. Practical is not pulling a Bentley or Maserati up to a Section 8 housing development. Practical is not even wearing an outfit one time, and buying something new because you have posted it to social media already! Hello, somebody! You have to know how to switch it, change it, and rearrange it. Ladies you would be surprised at how far the same top can take you when matched with a different bottom, and maybe a kimono. My ladies know what a good kimono can do! Fellas, you all have it a bit easier when it comes to wardrobe. All you have to do is switch out the shoes, put on a jacket, and throw on a different cap or hat, and you are good to go. So let's all try to ease up on "keeping up with the Joneses." It will allow our individuality to show through, and keep some coins in our pockets too!

I am sure that we all agree that life can happen to the best of us, and we may fall on hard times that may cause us to rob Peter to pay Paul at times; that's not what I am saying here. What I am saying is to consider having a practical and legacy building mindset. Have a mindset that will carve you out from the crowd, and a mindset that will keep more money in your stocks, real estate and insurance policies than in the cash registers. Keep in mind that individuals with a legacy building and practical mindset, who happen to fall on hard times, have the mindset to get back on track without really missing a beat. Because it's all in the mind!

Millionaires and billionaires didn't attain this overnight. Many times, these individuals have always been about the business of entrepreneurship from early on. They may have permed or cut hair out of their dorm rooms in college to earn extra money, or saved a portion of their earnings every payday to finally put a down payment on a starter home. These individuals never spend every dime they have frivolously. There is always a stash for a rainy day. Millionaire mindset individuals are good at networking and developing relationships that will be instrumental in them reaching a predetermined goal. They monitor their credit on a consistent basis, and pay their bills on time—they have financial literacy. So guess what, if these sorts of individuals happen to take a risk that turns out not to be favorable, they know how to start their cycle over again until they are back in a position of prosperity.

The Road Less Traveled

Take some time to research some of the most successful billionaires, such as Warren Buffett, Oprah Winfrey, Bill Gates, and

Mark Zuckerberg. You will be surprised at some of their stories, and how they achieved billionaire status. In the February 12th, 2020 Business Insider article, it noted that out of the 607 billionaires in the United States, only 5 of them are African-American (Jay-Z, Michael Jordan, Oprah Winfrey, David Steward, and Robert F. Smith, who is the richest African-American male in the United States, and who pledged a $34 million-dollar gift to pay off the student loans of Morehouse College 2019 graduating class). Once you research these individuals, and read their unique stories, you will see that it wasn't luck for them—it was mindset and motivation. You too can be in that number of mindset and motivation.

So, don't get caught up trying to put on for your city, your culture, your friends, your family, your job, etc., in an attempt to be accepted or "appear" to have it together. We have to get caught up in striving to leave behind a legacy for our children and our communities. We have to be okay with who we are, why we are, where we are, and what we have. If you are practical enough to have a Birkin bag or Benz, don't talk about the Kate Spade or Kia that your friend-girl has. Perhaps she is operating in her lane and exercising practicality. Her bank account just may shock you if you were to take a peep! Just something to think about.

Don't go into a career just because it is what your mother, father, sister, or aunt wanted to see you do. Go into a career that sits well with your spirit; one that will provide you with the tools and resources that you need in order to accomplish the dreams you have set out for yourself, anad assist you in reaching your purpose. One of my favorite sayings is, "Be a flamingo in a flock of pigeons." A pigeon is a little, plump, gray bird with purple and green coloring at the neck, and its head has a bobbing motion when it walks. A flamingo is a tall, elaborate, bright pink bird that feeds on living organisms in the water. If you ever see a flamingo standing in a flock of pigeons, you will not have to guess which one is the flamingo. The flamingo becomes very interesting because it does not look or act like the other birds, yet it is in the midst of the other birds.

This is what I have always aspired to do: not look or act like everyone else around me, but be myself regardless of who likes me or not—to take the road less traveled, and to carry myself in a way that is not based on the opinions or feelings of anyone else, but on the laurels of my God above, and by the meter of my own limitations. Once we accept our unique beauty, embrace it, and live in it, we will begin to truly evolve into the person that we were created to be. We will then be on the path to begin to discover our true purpose.

Each of us has a unique purpose, a unique assignment that will aid in that "Well Done" report from our Higher Power. We were not all created to be entrepreneurs, doctors, presidents, politicians, dancers, actresses, teachers, airline pilots, rappers, engineers, make-up artists, or CEOs. Your gift is unique to you and only you. The best part about it is that no one can ever take your gift from you—it's yours—it's in your bones, in your heart, and in your spirit. Your gift comes easy—it flows like water, it is natural, it is freeing, it is passionate, it is energy, it is a high vibration, it is you—and guess what? The light that will radiate from your gift is priceless!

<u>Circle the One That Doesn't Belong</u>

In kindergarten, I remember a lesson where the teacher gave us a sheet of paper with similar things, and we had to circle the one that did not belong. It was one of my favorite assignments to do. I was always so eager to find the one that did not belong. To me, the one that did not belong always stood out because there was something about it that did not match the others. In life, we have to be that something. There should be something about you that does not match others in the most positive, creative, and self-actualizing way. Allow life to circle you out from everyone and everything else on its canvas, and draw a ray of light around you that will guide others out of darkness if they are experiencing shadows. You will have earned yourself a better chance of influencing those around you when you stand out with your unique story that is authentic to you; a story that may change someone's life and free them from self-sabotaging outcomes.

Okay, I want to take another point of personal privilege here, if I might. This piece is a transparent journey, written to inspire at least one person to begin to shine from the inside out. As we discuss what it means to be uniquely us, let me point out that self-reflection is key! After my divorce, I did a LOT of self-reflection; I didn't jump into dating, living a "wild" life, or "turning all the way up" as some of us would say or even do. And if that is your thing, that is totally your prerogative. Do what is best for you! I am not here to judge anyone, but only here to share my journey, and habits that benefited me along my path of light and love. Now of course, I went out with friends to enjoy myself from time to time, but I wanted to be a better version of myself. I was in a focus-driven mindset; thus, I eliminated some things from my life, and added some things to my life.

After my separation, I began to eliminate anything or anyone who no longer aligned with my purpose. I eliminated non-value added behavior and replaced it with value-added behaviors. Value-added behaviors are behaviors that increase and elevate your purpose, and propel you toward your goals at lightning speed. Before you know what behaviors will add value, you must know your purpose, and to know your purpose you must consider your why and your value system. Because I had discovered my why, and had redefined my value system, I knew what activities and behaviors were value-added and non-value added. I knew the character of people that were value-added and non-value added. For me, value-added behaviors were engaging in healthy eating habits and exercise to ensure that my body was functioning at its best potential; meditating and reflecting on deep rooted challenges inside of myself that were the motive behind certain challenges to keep showing up in my life; listening to positive and uplifting sermons and podcasts; traveling to allow for a renewal and rebirth of my spirit; and making the decision to finally write this book and start my own business and non-profit. Thus, I began attending seminars and forums that would give me the tools that I needed to accomplish these things, as well as surrounding myself with like-minded people that were either doing the things I wanted to do, or heading in the direction that I sought. These are just a few examples of some of the activities and behaviors I put in place that would add value to my life and my future goals, and they have all paid off, and continue to pay off.

<u>Time-Out</u>

As much as I may have wanted a companion at times after my divorce, I chose myself and my spiritual Father as my companions. I used that time to truly pour into myself, to embrace all of my uniqueness, to love every inch of me. It is so easy to get caught up in seeking validation from anything and anyone besides our own selves. But this time is extremely necessary. Trust me! During this time, I learned so much about myself. Most importantly, I learned how to love myself the way I should have been loving myself all along. Loving every inch of me meant learning to say no to things that I really didn't want to do. Loving myself meant accepting my flaws, both physically and non-physically. Loving myself also meant saving my body, and not sleeping around with anyone and everyone to make up for lost time.

I was in a space to solely focus on myself, to do things in a way that would yield favorable results, and push me toward full alignment with my Father's will for my life. Thus, I eliminated sex from my life after my ex-husband. I did not want any distractions— nothing that would deter me or pull me away from becoming my best self; nothing that would create a soul-tie and prevent me from becoming who I know I was called to be. On top of that, I have an old-school mentality when it comes to intimacy. My body is EXTREMELY valuable, and not to be handed out like samples in the food court to fill the pleasure curiosity of someone walking by, to sample and taste like an open Sam's Club, and if they don't like it, throw it in the trash on the way out the door. So I chose to be abstinent until I met the man that would be deserving of my body, through his alignment and obedience with God.

My spirit was such that the man who would be deserving of my body would be in full alignment with my purpose, and serve to contribute in making me a better person than I already am, and vice versa. Someone who would aid in my inner light shining brighter than ever before, by advancing my assignment. Someone who would come by revelation, and not by manipulation. Someone who would draw me closer to my Higher Power, and not pull me away. Someone who would be vibrating on a high-frequency that matches mine, to the point where his goal would be to create a forever frequency together, withstanding any test of time. Someone who is being prepared by a Higher Power, just as I am. This person, I can't explain. I would only know it is him when I meet him.

If you have ever been divorced, or even if you have just come out of a committed relationship, take the time to yourself that you need! There is no rush to connect yourself with someone just to "appear" like you have it going on, or to prove a point, or to poise for social media. You will only open up the road of vulnerability. Singleness is not a curse—trust me! It is a blessing. It is a time to develop a wholeness; a single person is a whole person, contrary to popular belief. There is so much to be learned through singleness, and you will need every ounce of it when you do join yourself to another, with the end result being two whole individuals.

Supply and Demand

Love and companionship can be, and is, a beautiful thing! Everyone should experience love and companionship! Especially under the right context. When done in alignment with its true purpose, it fulfills earthly purpose. I am a very affectionate person! I believe we were created for the purpose of intimacy with another. Thus, the man that would be worthy of my body and the frequency in which it operates will embody these characteristics genuinely, and will be able to operate for a lifetime, and not just the meantime or in-between time—nothing more, or nothing less.

After my divorce was final, I decided I was ready to at least entertain a date every now and then. So, I went on a few dates with this one particular guy that I had met while out one day with my family on a trip to New Orleans, not realizing this person happened to live in Atlanta as well. He was there on business, and I on pleasure. We had chemistry, attraction, butterflies, and all of that. We enjoyed great conversations. He owns a prospering business, and overall came across very much like someone I would be interested in getting to know better. After 2 months of dating, he brought up being intimate sexually. I stated my piece, of not engaging in sexual intercourse during that time, and unfortunately, it wasn't where this particular person was at the time. This is where the true intentions of a person are always revealed. Arrogantly, he boldly expressed that if he did not get it from me, then he would get it from someone, as that is how he connects to someone, through intercourse! I thought to myself, "You go right ahead then, playboy—get it from whomever you feel you need to get if from but it will not be me. Knock yourself out." It blew my mind as I was thinking to myself, "Did this statement really just come out of a grown man's mouth?" But I quickly realized it was a grown boy speaking, that I had assumed was a grown man.

We have to realize that grown boys can appear as grown men, but once you tear away the pretty wrapping paper, and get down to the contents of the box, you realize what you are working with. I told myself, "If this is what I have to look forward to in dating after divorce, then I may have to be okay with remaining single!" The nerve of him! It was his honest response. I respected it, but I didn't agree with it, and that's okay. I appreciated the transparency as it allowed me to make a decision to move on without wasting any time on someone that was only out for pleasure and gain, and didn't care what came out of his mouth. He clearly wasn't the one God had for me. The one thing I did after my divorce was pray that God would go before me in all situations, to guide me and give me a level of discernment that would, without question, steer me in the direction of His will. We have to remember that our God is not the author of confusion but the author of clarity. In this situation, I was true to myself, my energy, my vibrations, and my values.

Three weeks later, this same person called me to apologize, and compared me to a "rare jewel"—his exact words. He voiced how rare it is to find a woman who values herself enough these days, and appreciated my choice to respect my body. Talk about being uniquely you! I was very appreciative of this gesture, but it also showed me that men, no matter the age, no matter how professional they appear, or no matter your choice, would still test you to see how far they could go with you. Don't let anyone test drive you! You are valuable, and there is a price that will be paid for value—no discounts given. When someone walks into the Mercedes Benz dealership to purchase that S550, there are no discounts. The car costs what it costs. And if they are not prepared to pay for it that day, guess what? They are escorted right off of the showroom floor, and outside through the sliding double doors. No negotiating. No gimmicks. You must treat your body the same way. If someone comes into your life, and they are not prepared to value you for what you are worth, then you need to politely escort them to the exit door of your life. Bye-bye and good day!

What I also realized by a response such as, "If you don't give it to me, I will get it from someone else," is that there are many women out there who are truly selling themselves short. We must realize that we will be treated as we carry ourselves. As Pastor R.C. Blakes once stated, we can't cook hamburgers in the kitchen and then advertise chicken; wondering why everyone coming is ordering chicken wings instead of hamburgers. Regardless of how desperate or in need of a companion we may be, we have to stop and think about what we are doing and why we are doing it. We have to consider the consequences of our behaviors, and be ready to be accountable to whatever the outcome is. Whether the outcome is a soul-tie, an unwanted pregnancy, an STD, or a headache, we must own it. We must also own who we are, and stop settling for less than God's best. Once we make up our minds that we are more than what's between our legs, our value rises. It's supply and demand. If what's between your legs is readily available, there is more supply than demand, and no one wants it. If there is more demand than what is being offered, the value goes up, as you now become rare. This person tried it with me, tried it, but it didn't work. You have to know your worth, and then add tax!

<u>Look Both Ways Before Stepping Out</u>

I have no doubt that my God has gone before me in all situations since my divorce. He has protected me from a couple of situations that were sure to lead nowhere. The lessons learned in my marriage were excellent teaching moments; and trust me, I definitely lean on these priceless lessons when necessary. In addition, the miracles, signs, and wonders that He will show us will give us chills if we ask Him.

Living in Atlanta, and probably anywhere in the world for that matter, you would be surprised at the number of prominent people, both men and women, with successful businesses, children, wealth, etc., wearing a mask of integrity, proclaiming to fear God, but who are truly wolves in sheep's clothing, hiding behind a fake persona, and only out to fulfill their own agenda—until they meet someone who can see through all the smoke. This is when the mask falls off, and the true colors of deception surface. Individuals can only hide who they are for so long. I say 6 months to a year max—but who has that sort of time to waste?! NO ONE! Many times, the goal for these individuals is to see how much they can gain from you before the mask falls off. That is why it is so important to ask the right questions, observe, take things slow, remain true to who you are, respect yourself, and not thirst after someone for the sake of jeopardizing your peace, your integrity, and your value—for if you do, you will be no better than them. For the good book states, if you wallow with pigs, you will get up covered in mud.

For accountability purposes, we have to be very careful of who we are attracting into our lives and why. This requires soul searching, observation of others, experience, and wisdom. In order not to repeat the same mistake twice, we must learn from our past experiences and recognize similar behavior or signs that would indicate someone is pretending to be someone that they are not. Now that is a topic for another book, but I say all this because, whether you realize it or not, being uniquely you has more shine than trying to blend in, or be accepted for fear of rejection, or what someone else thinks of you. Whatever your uniqueness is, don't sacrifice it just to please another. Many people that you are trying to please barely know if they are coming or going. So, learn from past mistakes; don't try to be someone you are not, and don't get so caught up in the hype or the "Joneses." Believe in yourself and in the power that you hold. When you find this power, and realize you have had it the entire time, you will now be on fire, and ready to Stay in Your Light!! Trust me; it is MIGHTY!

So be UNIQUE, be KIND, and let your light shine!

Shine Check:

This might have been a tough shine habit for some of you to get through, but trust me; it is a necessary shine habit. There is something for us all to learn from being uniquely ourselves. Take some time to think through the following questions, and jot down your answers in your favorite journal.

Name 3 situations in which you wanted what someone else had. What reasons do you feel you wanted these things?

List 5 characteristics that are truly unique to you. What makes these characteristics unique to you? How can these unique characteristics contribute to your purpose?

Have you ever jeopardized your value or your worth at any point in your life? Why? How would you now, after reading this shine habit, do things differently? How does that make you feel?

Notes

Shine Habit 4
Kindness Is the Ultimate Killer

"The highest form of wisdom is kindness."
– The Talmud

Why do we find it so hard to display acts of kindness to someone who may have betrayed us, hurt us, or crossed us in some way? A good friend of yours, whom you have known for years, tries to sabotage your name for personal gain; a road rage driver rolls their window down and calls you every name in the book of swearing; a significant other betrays you and deceives you in the most unimaginable manner; a co-worker makes sly innuendo comments to you, as if you can't read in between the lines—and every neuron in your body wants to fire off with each one of these hypothetical circumstances. But instead, you pray for these people. You offer to lend them a hand with something. You smile and say, "Have a blessed day on purpose," or one of my favorites, "Bless your heart." You may be saying to yourself, "Maybe that is what you do, but I would never lend a hand to someone who has wronged me? Are you crazy?!" And you know what? I get it! It's human emotion. But we must take a step back and ask ourselves, "What am I gaining from holding this grudge?" And you will find that the answer is "nothing." It is quite easy to throw stone for stone when we are hurt—that is the easy thing to do. But the more difficult thing to do is to treat that same person with kindness, and with a love that is so foreign to how we are used to handling situations, that it seems nearly impossible. I know it sounds hard to do, but the amount of peace and amount of light that will radiate from you, would be enough to turn a vampire into a hummingbird.

Now for the record, let me just say that it takes a lot of work and trial and error to get to this space of showing undeserving kindness in angering situations. It is not an innate characteristic, but it is one of the top traits to have. Another one of my mother's sayings is, "Kindness will break bones." It's the type of trait that will leave a question mark in the heads of those who thought they were getting under your skin. These are my favorite people to display kindness to, because I know it is what they lack. What better way to allow your light to shine from the inside out than by extending kindness to someone who is so undeserving of it. This is called true and genuine peace with oneself, but—believe it or not—most of us are not at peace with ourselves fully and honestly. We may say that we are, but are we really? Whether you are seeking attention from someone or something, trying to win a popularity contest amongst your friends or family, envious of the next person, or you allow others to think for you, you are not at peace with yourself. Your validation comes from an outside source as opposed to from within, but that's what this journey is about—learning to shine from the inside out. So I would like to share a few ways in which you can become successful at killing someone, or a situation, with kindness via the **S.T.O.P. phenomenon**.

S.T.O.P Phenomenon

Silence

We must all silence that voice that wants to react in a negative manner. Close your eyes, and take 10 slow, deep breaths, and fully reflect on what was said or done to you, or done to someone close to you, that has you ready to act a fool. Sometimes the best reply is no reply at all. Not everything deserves an immediate response. This is where many of us mess up. We feel as if we have to give someone a piece of our minds, speak our truth, not back down, or let someone have it. I use to feel like I had to respond immediately to someone after being wronged. I would pick up the phone, and then hang it up; or write a long text message, and then delete it. What I now do is not respond at all, and give myself that time to think before I respond. No one deserves that type of energy from us.

Now there is nothing wrong with speaking our truth, but there is a manner and time in which to do so. My Father above tells us, "Peace be still." So before giving a reply, if any, quiet your spirit, see if a response is warranted, and then proceed with a reply that does no harm. This is where you come in with the "slow kill." Most people cannot understand you when you come from this angle. They can't read you. You have your poker face on. You do not feed or entertain that desire in the other person to get under your skin. Whether we realize it or not, we let the other person know that we are bothered by them when we fire off, or speak without thinking. This is exactly what they want from us—our energy! We don't have to go tit for tat with anyone. Take the higher road!

The Light of My Shadows

I can recall a situation in which I was completely taken aback by someone who is a sorority sister, and a social friend of mine. Now granted, we were not best friends, but we hung out in very close mutual circles, knew each other's families, and had celebrated and supported each other during certain special occasions. I had even been there for this person during a major unexpected medical emergency, and we would just have fun when we were around each other. However, out of the blue, this person began to say very mean and negative things about me, and against my character, to a few other people in our mutual circle, which caught me by extreme surprise! They were things that were clearly not true, but the person to whom this individual was bringing the information back to, was closer to me, and relayed all that was stated by this individual. Keep in mind, I am talking about extremely mean and hurtful things that I would NEVER even utter out of my mouth about anyone, nor did I embody those characteristics—that's just the class in me. But because I am fully aware of my character, as are so many other people that know me very well, I didn't allow this to bother me one bit. I learned a long time ago that if a person can't find anything against you, they will make up something for the attention or relevance they seek; or to try to tarnish who you are. I learned that people will not like you for their own premeditated reasons. It could be anything from the way you carry yourself, to what you do, to what you have, to how you walk, to the husband you choose to marry, to the relationships you may have with others that may be envied, to how you eat your food, etc. Whatever the issue is, there is an underlying agitation that you unfortunately cannot resolve for them.

Kindness is The Ultimate Killer

So what did I do in this situation, you may be wondering? Well, I first wanted to know what the other individual's reply was when the negative comments were brought to them, as this person was extremely close to me. I have learned in life that it is not about who's real to your face, but about who is real behind your back. So I needed to understand this first and foremost. Once I had this understanding, and it was a favorable reply, I had a conversation with the individual that had stated the negative information, in which all that was stated was immediately retracted, with a default reason of, "I had a lot of family issues going on at that time, and have been going through a lot." Not sure what any of that had to do with me, but instead of stooping to a level that would have done more harm than good, I stated my peace of how I felt about what was said, listened to what this person had to say, and I said a prayer for this person. Unfortunately, I lost all trust and respect for this person, but I still operate in kindness and mutual respect when in the same space. Kindness will go much further than an ill spirit ever will! Trust me!

As a little girl, I used to say, "Sticks and stones may break my bones, but words will never hurt me." How true! The tongue is sharper than the sword, but sometimes we have to let some things roll off our backs like duck feathers, pray for those that have wronged us, and watch how karma stands up for us. Karma is like a rubber band. We can only stretch it so far before it come back to smack us in the face. We have to remember what our road map tells us: "Vengeance is mine," says the Lord—and so it is!

Time

Time heals all wounds! It may not feel like it at first, but I am a witness to this. When I first heard this statement, I thought it was very cliché, until after more than a few traumatic life events occurred with me. The pain that comes from any tragic life event brings with it such a level of confusion that you don't see the concept of time fitting in at all. Time seems so distant when you are in the throes of dark shadows. After my divorce, it was a year and a half before I even spoke a single word to my ex-husband, despite the numerous calls, texts, and voicemails left by him for an entire year wanting to reconcile. Not that I was upset or bitter, I just had no words, period, until I felt I was ready to respond. Reconciliation definitely was not even a thought in my head.

Time is necessary in many situations in which harm or an unkind act was done to you. You realize after time has passed that you don't even think about it anymore, or better yet, if you happen to think about it on a rare occasion, it holds no weight. The emotions you may have felt during that time have subsided. Your energy is completely different. Your environment is completely different. Your circle may even be completely different. During this time of reflection, you ask your Higher Power for a renewed spirit, to give you the words to speak if you were to ever encounter the person who may have wronged you, and you would be surprised at what the outcome will be.

Time allows for almost a detoxification of any negative feelings or vibes to flee. Through readings, experience, prayer, and wisdom, I have learned that by holding onto unfavorable feelings, grudges, and unforgiveness, we only do ourselves a disservice.

We continue to cloud our spirits with shadows, which only keeps us in a state of low energy. Once we are able to have time to reflect, detox, and forgive, we open up a light within us, which allows us to move forward on a high frequency, creating an avenue for continuance of blessings, new opportunity, and positive encounters. The easy thing to do is hold onto a grudge and give energy to a person or situation that is irrelevant. The hard thing to do is walk away, forgive, smile, and lean on your Higher Power for justice.

So always remember, just like a fine wine, everything and every situation gets better with time!

Opportunity

There is a time and a place for everything under the sun. After you have silenced yourself, and given it some "time," sometimes you have to wait for the right opportunity to return a favor of kindness when an injustice is served by someone, or just to even address it. Trust that the opportunity will present itself sooner or later. Many times, you don't even have to go searching for the opportunity. The way karma works, time and space will align itself so that the right opportunity is placed in front of you. So there is no need to go on a mad hunt for it. Also, using the **S.T.O.P. phenomenon** allows you not to burn bridges you may need to cross again. This is extremely important in petty situations that are really not that serious. And we all know that some of us are fans of petty! The same person who wronged you may need you for something one day. And this just may be the opportunity that karma has presented. The way our God is set up, He will always get the glory to turn something that was meant for bad, into something good (Genesis 50:20).

So just sit back and allow the opportunity to present itself, in which you will be able to radiate your light all over someone who served you that injustice. This is the biggest revenge. To show someone that although they may have committed an unfavorable act against you, you are favored so much that your spirit can turn an injustice into a justice. Sometimes you have to shine your light so that others may find their way. Your example of turning the other cheek may be just what is needed to have someone else reflect on their unfavorable actions, and how their acts did not harm you the way they meant them to. How special that we are made in His image, so much so that if we are loving our neighbors as ourselves, we allow others to see Him in us! How beautiful! Just rely on space and opportunity, and let the rest work itself out. Don't say I didn't warn you!

Positivity

So as you think, you will surely be. This may be hard for some, and I still have to catch myself with this one. I am not perfect by far—I am perfectly imperfect. If we try to remain positive in situations that are not so positive, we are already ahead of the game. So in those hurt situations, try to remain positive the best you can, and hope for a favorable outcome. It's hard when you want someone to feel hurt because you are hurt. As the saying goes, "Hurt people hurt people," but let me just add that "empowered people empower people." So, in an attempt not to hurt someone in your process of hurt, surround yourself with people who will help you reflect positively, and empower you. You don't need someone with a *"If that was me, I would have done"* type of persona. That mentality will only breed more darkness and negative energy—and can sometimes get people hurt. You need a *"I know it hurts now, but trust me, it will not always feel this way; come on, let's go grab a drink, or catch a movie"* type of vibe. These people take your mind off of the hurt, and buy you that "time" we talked about earlier in this shine habit. This is the type of tribe that you need; a tribe that is completely vested in your best interest. We will get into "tribes" a bit more in the next shine habit; however, we all need that friend or that person who will tell us what we need to hear, and not what we want to hear.

Also, remain positive that while you may not have the same relationship moving forward with the person who wronged you, you may be able to get to a cordial space, or a space in which you can operate in the same space, or even exchange small conversation. Being a member of a sorority, I have encountered this on a few occasions. I love my sorority dearly, but we all know that when you have an all-female organization of like-minded, high-achieving women, with colorful personalities, everyone will not always agree. So, I have had to remain positive in situations where a sister of mine may have said something not so nice about me to someone else, or disagreed with something I may have said in an inappropriate manner. I have learned not to argue or go back and forth with ANYONE. It is not that serious; plus, an onlooking person may not be able to figure out who the fool is. We have to state our peace in a firm and direct way, and move on. When we know who we are, and WHO we belong to, there is no reason to go back and forth. We have to learn to listen and observe more than we speak. It goes a long way!

Another important lesson to remember is that some people were brought into your life to teach a very important lesson, during a very important time in your life. So never regret a situation, as more so than not, it taught you something that you needed or will need along your journey.

Remember the one guy that I told you I dated seriously after my divorce? Well, this was a huge lesson and a blessing in disguise. It was a test to determine if I had learned the lesson meant to be learned from my marriage. We ended up reconnecting and dating for 5 months after the initial encounter, after what seemed as if Jesus had turned himself from a spirit back into the flesh, and had come down to speak to him personally—completely different behavior than the first encounter. He was a successful person in his own right, making it known on numerous occasions that his mother taught him Christ, and his father taught him hustle. I took an interest in his endeavors to support minority owned businesses, and to support someone I thought was a genuine person. After he took me to meet his family, and after he met mine, things began to weirdly shift at the 5-month mark. I told myself that I would do things opposite of what I did in my marriage. I would be extremely observant of red flags, and not tolerate anything that went against my morals, values, or standards. I said I would not go back and forth with anyone, but only observe and petition my Higher Power for His direction—and I am so glad I did.

We pray for people and things, but we have to keep in mind that the enemy hears our prayers as well. And in this particular situation, the enemy heard my prayer, and masked it as if it was of God. But nonetheless, I stood on my values, and I prayed for discernment. What I now realize is that this person mirrored me and played on what he thought I needed and wanted, for 5 months—even the second time around. After 5 months of dating, God began to reveal to me the very things I had prayed He would reveal. Little did I know that this person was far from whom he portrayed himself to be in public and in business, vs. everyday life. Time will always show us what a moment will not. So it serves all of us well to take things slow. The mask came off in every imaginable way, and in ways I would have never imagined—but I'm glad that it did. This situation re-enforced the meaning of the saying, *"When someone shows you who they are, believe them the first time!"*

Needless to say, this relationship ended abruptly, as quick as the close of a garage door going down, and I had no one to thank but my God, yet again. He granted me the protection of something not in His will, again! With no hard feelings, I wished him well under God's good graces and moved on with my life. I will never wish harm or ill-will on anyone. He will be perfect for someone seeking what he is offering; fortunately, I wasn't her and that's a blessing!

What this test showed me was that people that are meant to be in your life will come by revelation and not by manipulation, and not to be detoured by distractions that come dressed as attractions. Tests will come our way; we just have to be prepared when they come. Not everyone is meant to go the entire journey with us, but to teach us a valuable lesson, or to present the test that we need in order to move on to the next level once the test is passed. Just because someone doesn't go the journey with us, doesn't mean we have to slow down. We should keep our pace and our head to the sun, for when our head is to the sun, the shadows will fall behind us.

We have learned in this shine habit something that we all probably learned as a child: to treat others the way we want to be treated—with kindness—and when someone shows you who they are, believe them. By exercising the **S.T.O.P. phenomenon**, we allow ourselves the space, time, opportunity, and positive energy to assist us in killing with kindness. Remember, you just may be the motivation that someone needs, to shift their behavior from dark to light!

Always remember… "Positive Vibes Only!"

Shine Check:

Think of a time when you may have come out of character with someone in the most hurtful way because of something said or done to you. What behavior did you display? Did the situation escalate or de-escalate? Why?

If the situation escalated, what caused it to escalate? What caused it to de-escalate?

What specific actions under the **S.T.O.P. phenomenon** could you have utilized to prevent coming out of character, or to de-escalate the situation?

Have you ever used the **S.T.O.P. phenomenon** without realizing it? What was the outcome?

Notes

Shine Habit 5
Positive Tribes...Positive Vibes

"Be the energy you want to attract...
and watch what happens."

Now this one seems like a no brainer, right?! Wrong! Why is it that so many of us continue to entertain negative Nina's, mumbling Michelle's, angry Ashley's, and prideful Paul's?! Have you ever noticed, when you are around these types of people, that they suck all the energy and life out of you? Their problems become your problems. Their energy becomes your energy. It's because it's really true! Just because you are positive, upbeat, and radiating happiness, doesn't mean that others around you feel the same way, and that's perfectly okay. I am not here to tell anyone how to behave, but I am here to guide you on how you can be a light in the midst of negative energy, how to radiate positive energy to attract positive people, and how to politely excuse yourself once you realize your vibrations are being lowered at the cost of someone else's darkness.

Two of the most important pieces of advice I ever received regarding people were, "You are the company you keep," and, "Don't ever let anyone move you off of your rock." Your rock is your safe zone. It is where you are grounded and secure; where your foundation is cemented, and where your light is the brightest. We cannot ever give anyone that type of power over us, to remove us from our safe zone. We must wish them well with the energy of love and light, and move on. Some people that you may think are your "friends," are only there to suck you dry—like a mosquito hovering over a Louisiana bayou. You have something they want. The energy and light you possess is what they seek to drain from you to lift them up. Then there are some friends that are genuinely in your life to walk with you, support you, and help you to carry your cross. These are the people that truly mean you well, and will, more likely than not, walk with you your entire journey of life.

<u>Spring Cleaning</u>

Along our paths of life, we have met, been introduced to, grew up with, lived with, fallen out with, argued with, and dismissed people from many walks of life. Some people are for reasons and seasons, while others are meant to be there until the end—and guess what? That is okay. Through life experiences, I have learned that you have to be very selective about the company you keep. And for good reason. All company is not good company, and all company is not bad company. We have to know the difference. I had to learn the difference. And what is that difference, you may ask? It is a question I had to ask myself and ponder over honestly. To begin to understand this very important statement, we must understand that we are each unique (as we just journeyed through in the previous shine habit). Just because someone is not like you, doesn't make them a bad person. We each live off of our own personal likes, dislikes, desires, values, and goals. But one thing that should be common amongst our tribes is that there is always a light, not darkness, that radiates from their inner spirit—the key words here being "inner spirit." When our tribe walks with an aura of light that comes from within them, the light that radiates from them will always be there to cast out any shadows that may be creeping into our space, if we ever happen to descend into a dark place.

Our tribe should be able to lift us up when we are down, without letting the world know that we were even down. A positive-light tribe walks in a no-judgement zone. It's a place we should be able to go and recharge our battery. Just like those electric cars that pull into a parking space to charge up, that's what our tribe should do for us. If your tribe is not doing this for you, ladies and gentlemen, you may want to reconsider your tribe and what their true value is in your life. I am not afraid to say that I have lost people I thought were in my tribe, along my journey. We are not here on earth to hoard people like we do old clothes and things jammed into our closets, which we know we should have gotten rid of a long time ago. We get to choose who we decide to roll with on this side of heaven, so I caution you to choose wisely. Like the old saying goes, "If the shoe doesn't fit anymore, get rid of it"— because it no longer has purpose for you. If you try to squeeze into them, you may end up with corns and hammertoes which causes pain. We don't have time for that. So, be selective in the relationships you develop—it's okay. It is not being bougie, high-maintenance, or "too much." Some individuals have purpose for a lifetime, and some we outgrow during a season. We get one shot at this ride, so why not make it worthwhile and live it in joy and positivity, with those who are complementary to our energy.

<u>Go with Those That Are Going with You</u>

Think back to when you were in elementary, middle, or high school. Do you remember your mother, father, or guardian pretty much selecting your friends for you? Or was I the only one? I was not allowed to attend sleepovers, or go anywhere with anyone whom my mother had not had a phone conversation with, met in person, or had known their family. It was how we were raised. My mother did not play that AT ALL! She wanted to ensure that the friends and people that were around my sister and I were people that were loving, family-oriented, positive, safe, supportive, and had our best interest, just as much as she did, if not more.

I was taught to ALWAYS go with those individuals that were going with me. In other words, what you give out to others, ensure that you are being reciprocated the same in return. If not, don't waste your energy on them. This statement could not be closer to the truth. How many times have we bent over backwards, stood up straight, and bent over backwards again for someone, whether it be family, a close friend, a boyfriend, or a companion, only to not benefit the same loyalty or kindness in return? More than a few, I am sure! How did it feel? Did it leave you with a positive feeling? Or did it leave you with a negative feeling? Whatever feeling it left you feeling, I am sure the feeling wasn't one that included a smile and a fuzzy feeling.

Many times, experience is our best teacher. Whatever we don't learn from our parents or guardians, we learn through experience. After we encounter enough opportunists, back stabbers, users, or beneficiaries along the way, the lessons of experience kick in really quick. We begin to tell ourselves things like, "I am not entertaining any new friends," or "My circle is very small." We learn that not everyone wishes us well, so we begin to cut people out of our space and our life. We begin to recognize the power of positive energy, and how those around us play a role in that. I am by no means telling you not to entertain any new genuine people in your life, but I am encouraging you to be wise, and to use discernment in spirit judgement.

Rule of Reciprocity

I am a strong believer in treating other people in the manner in which I would like to be treated, regardless of what anyone may have done to me! I know this may sound a bit crazy or naive, but it's the truth, and I am going to tell you why. Have you ever heard the saying, "How people treat you is a reflection of them, but how you respond is a reflection of you?" I live by this. One of the most gratifying feelings is one in which someone who has mistreated you or hurt you, doesn't get the satisfaction of you entertaining them on their level of ignorance or petty. Because, believe me, if they knew better, they would do better. So it is not your problem to address. We must allow people the space to understand themselves, and figure out (without our help) what is causing them not to know any better. Believe me, your response will be the determining factor between immaturity and wisdom. Choose wisdom!

We all have, in a moment of upset, spoken words to someone, that we probably wish we could retract. I know I have! Unfortunately, once spoken, those words are out, and may have already done damage that may be unfixable. So we have to learn to just kill with kindness, and allow those rays of light to bounce off of us. We must trust that the peace we will feel within us will drown out the negativity and misery that someone may be trying to suck us into.

Positive Vibe Traits

I would like to share a handful of **Positive Vibe Traits** that you can use in your everyday journey, which will allow you to begin to attract those positive tribes that will be sure to last a lifetime.

Speak Even When Not Spoken To

In all honesty, this is one of my pet peeves, to walk by someone or walk into a room, speak to someone, and the gesture is not returned. There are individuals I have encountered that act as if they are some kind of a Pharaoh sitting on a throne, and someone has told them that it is not appropriate to speak when spoken to. I was always raised to speak when I walk into a room full of people, or if I come into contact with someone. Call me Southern or just plain friendly, but in my most humble opinion, speaking is a sign of respect, politeness, and a signal that you are comfortable in your own skin. It's just plain manners! So I encourage you to extend the courtesy of speaking to those you come in contact with, regardless if you know them personally or not. Contrary to what you may believe, you just may be speaking to someone who may become a very close friend, someone whom you may be able to network with, or whom may just remember the politeness you showed them and extend a favor on your behalf.

It is documented that speaking or not speaking can sometimes be a cultural behavior, and that is perfectly fine; but in my educated opinion, speaking is extremely harmless. The worst that could happen if you speak to someone, is that the individual does not speak back. But you would have done your part, radiated a positive light, made your soul happy, and opened up the lines of communication to attract like-minded individuals. So, keep moving, as you are already ahead of the curve!

Be Kind

A kind spirit is extremely attractive! Who doesn't want to be in the presence of someone who is kind?! Kindness is like a magnet. I have even heard people say that they have gotten married to someone because they were just an extremely nice and kind person! Obviously there needs to be more in the equation if you are considering spending your life with someone; however, the fact remains that being kind is a sure trait to radiate a genuine light, and attract like-minded, positive people into your life. Have you ever had someone be a downright clown to you, but you killed them with kindness, which left them with no choice but to either apologize or switch their attitude? We just explored this in the previous shine habit! It's that supply and demand notion again. The more you feed an animal, the more they want to eat, right? So the more you entertain an unkind spirit, the more unkind they will be. However, the minute you don't throw stone for stone, or act out, you confuse the situation. Give yourself a round of applause! You didn't allow yourself to get sucked into the nonsense, so there is now a level of uncertainty of you on behalf of the other person. Because you gave off an unbothered persona, the energy shifts. These individuals now may want to get closer to you because of your personality, and because you carry a kindness that may be the balance to what they lack. This is what you want. Always kill an unkind spirit with kindness, and bury them with a smile!

Express Gratitude

Just in case you were wondering, a sincere thank you goes a long way! Oftentimes, we forget that no one is obligated to do anything for us. We tend to live in a "right here...right now...you owe me" society. But when you practice a simple thank you, for an act of kindness bestowed upon you, no matter how big or how small, you will begin to attract individuals who will want to support you, and who genuinely have your best interest. Gratitude comes in all shapes and sizes. It can be a simple thank you, voiced when someone gives you a compliment; a personalized hand-written thank you note to someone whom you want to feel extra special; a bouquet of flowers to your mom, just to remind her that you appreciate her support; or a home-cooked meal for your husband, to show appreciation for the many nights he may have taken you out to eat. It is acts such as these that will ensure that we keep continuous positive vibes around us, and will also plant seeds of reciprocity. We receive back what we give out. Again, it's called "karma." So, plant seeds of gratitude, and you will be sure to reap gratitude, and a few positive friends along the way!

Forgive

Now this is a concept that many of us struggle with. I had to learn forgiveness. I am still learning forgiveness. Forgiveness takes the 3 P's: patience, practice, and pardoning those who may have hurt us or wronged us in some capacity. Forgiveness is not always easy, depending on the magnitude of the injustice. However, I have learned through life experiences that forgiveness is more for the person who was hurt, not for the person who did the trespassing.

Forgiveness allows our inner spirit to be at peace; it allows for us not to be weighed down by burdens long after they have occurred. Forgiveness opens up an energy that is magnetic; it allows others to see Him in us. I don't know about you, but I cannot be around someone too long who harbors resentment for almost everyone that they see. Everybody has wronged them, and they are the victim. I think it is fair to say that in life we all will be hurt, will hurt others, and will be betrayed or mistreated a time or two or three—but this is not an excuse to think that everyone we come across will do the same to us.

One of the hardest things I have ever had to do in life was to forgive my dad, forgive my ex-husband, and forgive myself—believe me, it took a lot of praying and self-reflection. But at the end of the day, I had to forgive them, and forgive myself, in order to be able to move on, establish meaningful relationships, love, and position myself for future success. I could not use their behavior or circumstances as a crutch, or as a pity pass. I realized early on that I am responsible for my happiness, and as long as I have the Lord on my side, and forgiveness in my heart, I could move mountains! Because of my forgiveness, I was able to allow my dad to walk me down the aisle on my wedding day, which I struggled with at first. But I am so glad I did, as it was not only further healing for myself, but healing for all those around us who witnessed this moment.

So whenever you feel as if you are harboring a grudge for something someone has "done" to you, remember that our Lord is a forgiving God. He forgives us day in and day out. If we are made in His image, and we expect His grace and mercy, then we have to keep that same energy, and operate in grace and mercy in our dealings with others. It will free you, for life!

Shine Check:

In this shine habit, we discovered how our positive light can help attract and keep positive people around us. As a thought-provoking lesson, turn to a clean page in your journals. Make four separate columns on the page: Label the first column, Tribe; the second column, Value Added; the third column, Non-Value Added; and the fourth column, Benefit. In the first column, list the names of all the individual people that you consider a member of your "tribe." Give each person 10 lines in the columns. In the second column, list value added traits of the individual. In the third column, list non-value added traits of the person. In the fourth column, you will place a check if you have more value-added traits than non-value-added traits. At the end of the exercise, you will be able to clearly see who adds value and who does not. This is not to tell you to fire your tribe, but it will allow you to reflect on who is in your circle, and the richness that they each may bring, or not bring. At the end of the day, you want to ensure that you are surrounded by more value added, positive light individuals, than non-value added, negative light individuals.

Notes

Shine Habit 6

Vitamin N

"Wherever you go, no matter what the weather,
always bring your own sunshine."
– Anthony J. D'Angelo

I have always been fascinated by all of God's most wonderful creations around me. I remember as a little girl, I would always ask my mom, "Who created the earth, the trees, the sky, and all that surrounds us?" And she would reply, "God did, baby." Of course, that wasn't enough for me, so I would take it a step further. My next question was, "Well, who created God?" And she would never hesitate to say, "Baby, He just always was, and always will be." I didn't question this any further, and trusted what she told me to be true.

As I grew older and more mature, I realized how true this statement was. When we look at the sheer magnitude and energy captured in the universe, it is evident that this sort of power can only come from a supernatural, eternal, all-powerful, spiritual source. Genesis 1:1 note, "In the beginning, God created the heavens and the earth." In my humble opinion, this is one of the most powerful statements ever known to man. When we think about all that the earth encompasses, it is mind-blowing, yet calming all at the same time. The earth, in its rarest, purest form, has everything that we need to survive. It has air, water, plants, vegetation, fish, trees, sun, rain–you name it! These are all vitamins that nourish our very soul. Because God is the creator of all of these things, and God is peace and love, I experience peace and love when I am out enjoying these elements of nature that were placed here for us to enjoy. This is what I call my "Vitamin N," or my Vitamin Nature.

In the Natural State

It is quite evident that there are many individuals who are not "out-doorsy" people. These individuals would rather be inside, away from the sun, bugs, rain, heat, cold, and products of nature. I am not trying to persuade you otherwise. Nonetheless, I am here to provide insight on practices that you can choose to adopt, to shine from the inside out, specifically using natural elements, which will be discussed in this shine habit. I am not a huge astrology fanatic, but I do read to understand all phenomena. I am a Gemini, and am considered an Air sign. Air signs represent the breath of life. Air is a primary nutrient. Without it, none of us would be living. So conceivably, this correlates to the walks in the park that I enjoy, the dining on restaurant patios, cool breezes in the fall, and raised windows after a hard rain. I find so much peace in these activities. It is as if my spirit and energy is renewed, allowing my light to shine brighter.

Whenever I take long walks or go for runs in the park, or just sit outside taking in the sounds and smells, I am reminded of His goodness, His love, His mercy, and His grace. This reminds me that if our God can love us so much as to create an entire universe, complete with sustainable, eternal nutrients for us to survive on and enjoy daily, then I am in no shape, nor do I have the power to treat anyone less than me, give off a negative energy, or be mean-spirited. You may ask, "Well, how so? What does nature have to do with how you treat someone?" I am so glad you asked! The key word that I mentioned above is "love." You see, we each are made of dirt, water, air, and light. We were formed from mere dirt, and to dirt we shall return. We were formed from dirt and filled with water; air or breath was blown into us, and a light source was placed at our core, which is our spirits. This light source is the One whose image we are made in. Once we are able to understand our true source, we are able to grow and gain energy from that very source, allowing us to behave according to His image. His image does not operate negatively, or in a mean-spirit fashion, so why should we.

Think about this: Babies receive nourishment from the breast of their mothers; flowers and trees gain nourishment from the rain and sun; humans gain nourishment from vegetation, water, living wildlife, and sun—are we starting to see a relationship here? I sure hope so! The commonality here is that all living things gain supplementation from the same sources—the breast of the universe. Why not take advantage of these sources to bring out the best of who we are!

Riding the W.A.V.S.

Have you ever noticed that when we take care of our bodies, by drinking water, eating vegetables, getting fresh air, and lying out in the sun, we feel so good?! And what happens when we feel good? Our attitudes are more positive, correct? We are not as quick to get an attitude with others; we don't feel the need to put others down as to exude a certain level of control—our minds are clear, and our bodies are banging! We are able to give off a light that can only be gained from the one Source who has provided all of the elements for us to enjoy. This is the ultimate vitamin!

I want to share a few of my practices used to enjoy these elements, and how you, too, can incorporate some of these same habits into your daily or weekly routine. So, join me in riding the **W.A.V.S**!

Water

Water is one of the most vital nutrients there is. It makes up over 50% of our body weight, and is used by all of our cells, organs, and tissues to hydrate and regulate bodily functions. Have you ever had an extremely long and busy day, to the point that you did not even have one glass of water? What did you feel like? Were you in a good mood or headspace? Did you feel light-headed? Bloated? Cranky? Crampy? Ready to snap? Probably all of the above, right?! I know, for some people, drinking water is not the easiest thing to do all the time. Some of us have to have a piece of lemon, a powdered flavor, or something of the like in our water to drink it. I just happen to love water! I keep a water bottle on my night stand at home, several on my desk at work, and one in my car. It is extremely necessary in order to prevent dehydration and constipation, regulate temperature, make sure our skin is popping, and so on. Sometimes when I feel myself getting irritated by something, I grab a glass of water. It has a calming effect, allows time for me to regain my composure, and prevents something from being said out of my mouth that I might later regret. On the other hand, water is a stress relief. We all love the beach, right? Well, some of us do. Sitting and listening to the waves of the ocean is so peaceful! It allows time for reflection, and even provides mental clarity. Sometimes life puts us through the wringer, and we just need to get away so as not to become tight, bitter, or cold. Water will do this for us! It has a way about it that I am in love with! It gives me exactly what I need, to allow my best self to shine through, and perhaps it does the same for you as well!

<u>Air</u>

Earlier in this shine habit, I briefly mentioned that I am an Air sign. Air is the most critical element in nature—no air, no life—it's as simple as that. Air is found everywhere; it is invisible and cannot be contained. When babies are born, they are often tapped on their bottom to allow their lungs to fill with air, and to produce that initial cry. My favorite way to use air is to take deep breaths. Deep breaths are so extremely important for your body, mind, and spirit. Again, it is a great stress reliever when someone says the wrong thing to you; and it relieves pain, increases energy, lowers blood pressure, cleans your blood, keeps your lungs clear, and much more. Besides deep breathing, exercising is another great way to take in air, and lose pounds while doing so! Exercising is definitely a consistent part of my weekly routine, whether I am at the gym, training with my trainer, dancing samba, taking classes, or doing a quick workout at home. Through exercise, blood is pumping throughout our bodies, providing our muscles and cells with energy, and giving us a glow like no other. So, let's get those lungs working, and inner light shining, all at the same dang time!

Vegetation

The root of the earth! Vegetation is rich in so many different vitamins that sustain our everyday health. I am not going to labor on vegetation , as we all know that eating vegetables daily is important in providing nutrients, moving waste through our bodies, etc. If you are not a veggie eater, there are supplemental drinks, shakes, powders, and pills that would allow you to still benefit from vegetables, minus the taste. I am a protein and veggie girl. So, typically, my plate will consist of all protein and some sort of veggie. I love spinach, broccoli, Brussels sprouts, yellow squash, kale, cabbage, and many other fresh fruits and vegetables. I think this is what has worked in keeping me at a certain weight most of my life. I have a hard time with getting enough carbs, but I am working on that! I am not a huge fan of rice, potatoes, and pasta, although I do eat them sometimes. My mother did not serve us bread with every meal unless she cooked greens, and then she would make that good ole buttermilk cornbread! But vegetables were always present on our plates. Well-balanced meals were what my mother strived for, so veggies have always been a part of my everyday routine. I try to have vegetables or fruit with at least 2 of my 3 meals each day. Sometimes for breakfast, I may have only fruit; lunch may be a large salad, with protein; and dinner may be protein, vegetables, and a healthy starch. I do splurge and indulge in that spicy Popeye's fried chicken, chips, and queso, and fried seafood every now and again, but balanced meals are called balanced for good reason—it gives the body and mind balance as well! How good is our God, to provide us with everything we need to give us balance. And when our bodies and minds are balanced, everything else falls right into place. What a wonderful thing!

Sun

The sun is a bit tricky, or should I say a mixed blessing! I think our God wanted to test us when He created the sun! The sun is magnificent in all its wonders. It gives us light to guide our paths during the daytime, provides energy to growing trees and plants, warms our bodies, generates weather patterns, treats some eczema, regulates blood levels and circadian rhythms, and equally important, provides vital nutrients such as Vitamin D.

Have you ever heard the phrase, "If you can't stand the heat, stay out of the kitchen?" Well, guess what? The sun can be a kitchen for many people. Most people have a love/hate relationship with the sun. Either you love it, or hate it...and for obvious reasons, right?! Too much sun can be extremely detrimental to the body, and cause cancers, sunburns, rashes, heat stroke, and much more. So we must all understand how much sun is enough for our skin. Ideally, 10–30 minutes of morning or midday sun is recommended, but it really depends on how sensitive your skin is to sunlight. Darker complexions can handle much more sun without getting sunburns. Growing up, I was prone to heat rash. My face and lips would develop these tiny bumps, and my skin would take on a reddish hue. It was also extremely itchy! I went to see a dermatologist, who stated that I had some type of sun dermatitis. So I would use steroid creams to treat it. In my late 20s and early 30s, I realized that my skin no longer developed the bumps and redness when I went out in the sun. So whatever it was, it healed itself! Now I absolutely love the sun! I monitor my time in the sun, but the sun gives me so much life, and puts a smile on my face just by being out!

There are many benefits of the sun. It is a natural mood enhancer and "pick-me-upper." My favorite color is yellow, and for good reason! I have always been attracted to this color since I was a little girl. My favorite cartoon character was Tweety Bird! I had a big, life-sized stuffed Tweety Bird growing up, and believe it or not, I still have it somewhere in storage. One day, I decided to do a little research on this color, and some of the traits behind it. I was surprised to find that much of what this color represents, I embody! Yellow breeds a happy disposition, creativity, a critical attitude of self, perfectionist tendencies, methodical thinking, an independent nature, a tendency to hide emotions, spontaneity, good communication skills, and a modern outlook. These are all very true, and honestly, my perfectionist tendencies and my tendency to hide emotions was one of the major driving forces to write this book! Perhaps you too can research your favorite color to understand why you may be drawn to a particular color. The color characteristics just may surprise you!

As I got the nerve to write this book, I began to think about the years of my life. I realized that I have had many shadows that I have come out from under, to allow my inner light to begin to shine. There is a peace that happens with transparency and vulnerability—an awakening, or a shift, if you will. And it feels SOOO good! So, for me, the sun is a reminder of the light that I have inside of me despite my misfortunes, and all the brilliance and radiance that comes forth when I allow that light to reach people and places beyond myself.

Shine Check:

As we come to the end of riding the **W.A.V.S.** of Vitamin N, it is my sincere hope that there are a few nuggets that you can take with you, or incorporate into your routines, to allow that inner light within you to shine forth by using many of the natural elements that God has placed in this earthly realm for each of us to enjoy. I encourage you to do an internal check of your Vitamin N, by considering some of the questions below.

- What current activities do you enjoy that require the use of water, sun, and air? How do these activities make you feel when you engage in them?
- Are there any specific activities that you engage in when you feel irritated? Do you consider these activities to be healthy, and do they push you closer to your purpose? If any, what changes can you make?
- What small dietary changes could you make to begin to incorporate more water, fruits, and veggies into your routine, if you currently lack these vital nutrients?

Notes

Notes

Shine Habit 7

Serve Honey!

"You have not lived today until you have done something for someone who can never repay you."
– John Bunyan

As I pondered this shine habit, I couldn't help but think back to my first experience with lending a hand to support an effort that involved doing something for someone else. It was as early as 6 and 7 years old. Still living in New Orleans, I remember always wanting to run outside and help my downstairs neighbor (who was also the husband of my baby sister) pick up cans and cut the grass. Mr. Willie was his name, and we would spend about an hour picking up cans in the neighborhood, smashing them, and taking them to a place to recycle them for money. The older couple, who were like grandparents to me, also had a small evening job in which they would go and clean the office of one of the local physicians in Mid-City, New Orleans. I would not hesitate to run downstairs and hop in their red pick-up truck on the evenings that they had to go clean the physician's office. They were the private janitors for this physician, and I would be so excited to tag along and proceed to assist them in cleaning the office, sweeping, straightening up magazines, emptying trash, and wiping down the exam rooms. At the time, I had no idea the impact

99

of what I was doing to assist them, but I knew that in my heart, it felt really good.

Express Yourself

My mother worked for South Central Bell, which was the telephone company in New Orleans at the time. She was a Carrier Service Marketing Representative. Her job was a unionized job in which employees were under a legally binding contract, and could meet and negotiate with management over any issues that affected them and their jobs, such as wages, benefits, and working conditions. At about 4 or 5 years old, I remember my mother's job had a strike, in which the employees executed a concerted refusal to work for their employer. It was backed by the union to assert their right and protest a particular issue that was negatively affecting them. At this young age, I vividly remember going out on the "picket line" with my mother. A large group of employees walked in a circle in front of the building, carrying signs on wooden sticks, chanting the same message. I had no clue at that time what they were saying, nor the reasons behind what they were saying or doing, but I knew that my mother was chanting, so I began chanting as well. As I grew older and saw more and more picket lines, I did more research and asked questions to understand the meaning behind this parade of people all chanting the same thing. It was then that I learned that these people were fighting for the right to something that they did not have, which was necessary to execute in their job role. They were standing up for a right, and allowing their voices to be heard. So from an early age, I was exposed to lending a helping hand, and community activism.

It wasn't until I was in high school that I really became involved in community outreach and support. Having a sister that was diagnosed with Type 1 diabetes at an early age, I would volunteer for the Diabetes Walk every year with my family. I also would participate in the AIDS Walk in Piedmont Park, volunteer for Habitat for Humanity, and volunteer my time, talents, and efforts in numerous organizations within my high school. One of my favorite organizations in high school was a group named Nia Umoja, founded during my sophomore year. It was a group of mainly minority students who came together to advocate for cultural diversity and tolerance within our school. We would implement culturally diverse projects around the school, bring in guest speakers, conduct a Black History program in February, as well as many more activities. Being a member of the Keyettes and Beta Clubs also afforded me many opportunities to lend a hand in community support. All of these activities and efforts evoked a feeling of wholeness inside of me. It left me wanting to do more. It placed a smile on my face every time I saw the fruits of our efforts go forth. It brightened the light within me and expanded the will and the drive to want to do more to help others, and to advocate for things that would make a difference in the lives of those people not as fortunate.

Don't Forget Your Crown

Because of this passion that was born inside of me for community activism at a young age, and the wonderful feeling it gave me, I decided that I wanted to make a much larger impact, in a way that would ignite a fire inside of other young ladies that were my peers in my surrounding communities. My senior year in high school, I ran across a flyer that was posted near the gymnasium. It was a flyer for the 1998 Miss Black Teen of Atlanta Scholarship pageant. My first thought was fear. I had only competed in one pageant at that point in my entire life, and it was my high school's Miss CHS pageant, in my 9th grade year. I completely drew a blank during my talent as I stood to recite Maya Angelou's Phenomenal Woman. It was as if time stood still, and I could feel the blood flowing through each blood vessel attached to my body. I was thoroughly embarrassed and vowed that I would never ever do that again. But as fate would have it, I was encouraged and motivated by my past pageant mistake, and by my will to make a difference within the community on a larger stage. Thus, I told my mother of my desire to enter the Miss Black Teen Atlanta 1998 pageant, and she supported me 150%.

As mentioned earlier, my family had never owned a car, and up to this point, we still did not own a car. Nevertheless, I entered a pageant in which I would compete with high school girls from across the metro-Atlanta high school regions, in areas of talent, question/answer, and evening gown. Practices were scheduled on school nights at Therrell High School in Southwest Atlanta. My mother would ensure that I attended these practices; she hopped cabs, caught rides with other candidates that were competing against me, and rode MARTA. She did whatever she needed to do to ensure that I never missed a rehearsal. Due to my spoken word talent blunder in the Miss CHS pageant 3 years prior, I decided my talent would be a dance piece.

I had become intrigued with African-dance during my junior year in high school, and had taken some classes at a local dance studio that offered African dance. I fell in love with the dance, the movements, and the energy. One of my high school peers was an African drummer that did some drumming on the side outside of school. I humbly asked my peer if he wouldn't mind drumming for me during my talent portion as I performed an African dance for my Miss Black Teen Atlanta 1998 talent. To my surprise, he was more than thrilled to drum for me! So, at that point, I was feeling really good about it. I rehearsed my talent after school, at least 3 evenings out of the week, with the African drummer. I went to the fabric store and picked out the pattern I wanted for my dance costume, which consisted of a red, black, and gold African-print wrap skirt and head dress. I was so excited!

I wanted to ensure that I did the very best that I could in this pageant, since I would be competing against other young ladies from across other well-known metro-Atlanta high schools. For the stage question and answer component, I worked with an extremely gracious African-American female pageant coach who worked with me on spur of the moment questions. For my evening gown, I chose an all-white, full gown with a sequin bodice and a pale-yellow chiffon waist belt. It was absolutely gorgeous, and I fell completely in love with it! After about 4–6 weeks of rehearsals, it was finally pageant day. I competed against about 19 other young ladies from various metro-Atlanta high schools. Although nervous, I was extremely excited and humbled by the experience up to that point, and I felt in my spirit that it could only get better from that point forward. The pageant was held at the Georgia World Congress Center in downtown Atlanta. The audience was packed with people from all over Atlanta. Former Atlanta Mayor, Kasim Reed, was one of my pageant judges, although he had not run for Mayor, nor had been elected Mayor at that time. I will never forget the moment when I and a young lady from Collins Hill High

School stood as the last top two candidates on stage, right before my name was called as the new Miss Black Teen Atlanta 1998! My second runner-up was Jasmine Burke, who is now a well-known American actress whom have appeared in many films to include *Daddy's Little Girls*, *The Secret Life of Bees*, *Mississippi Damned*, and *Saints & Sinners* to name a few. Congratulations Jasmine on all of your accomplishments!

As I stood on stage, I think every nerve in my body went numb! I was utterly speechless. I could not believe that I had won a major pageant that would afford me scholarship monies to attend Spelman College, and a year platform of community service in which I would serve in nursing homes, speak at other high schools in the metro-Atlanta area, speak on the radio about my community efforts, and really just live out a year of a passion that I had worked so extremely hard to bring to fruition. My dream had come true! I had watched pageants on television as a young girl; I had admired pageant winners and queens for their poise, grace, inner beauty, and community platforms—and now I would be walking in those same shoes. I was getting ready to SERVE HONEY! This was the beginning of the beginning for me— for community efforts, for more pageant competitions, for new experiences—and I was ecstatic!

Serving, Sidelines, and Sorority

Winning the title of Miss Black Teen Atlanta 1998 was truly a humbling experience, and opened so many doors of opportunity in the years after. I went on to attend Spelman College, where I continued to volunteer my time with various walks across the city, campus service opportunities, and even had a work study job at Spelman's community service office to put a few extra dollars in my pocket that I didn't save from my refund check to live off of!

In my junior and senior years at Spelman, I ended up auditioning for the Atlanta Falcons Cheerleaders after seeing the ladies in a parade and on television. Unfortunately, I didn't make the team on my junior year audition, but after strengthening my dance skills by taking jazz dance classes at the Atlanta Ballet, and putting one of my favorite scriptures—Philippians 4:13, "I can do all things through Christ who strengthens me"—in my shoe, and dancing on it, I made the team in my senior year! This extreme accomplishment afforded me many opportunities to serve the Atlanta community and many other communities across the country on an exceptionally large scale. From making service appearances at the Atlanta VA hospital, children's hospitals, charity and celebrity golf tournaments, V-103 radio, Fox 5 News, TLC television network, and numerous parades, to performing overseas, in Greece, Italy, Egypt, and Portugal, for American troops stationed in those countries through the USO tours, I was able to further carry out my passion for service on an even larger platform, while doing what I love to do, which is dance.

After dancing and serving the Atlanta community for 7 years, I still had a passion to continue making a difference in the lives of others through service; thus, I was initiated into Alpha Kappa Alpha Sorority, Inc. a few years later, in which I get to carry forth my love for service to all mankind, as often as I choose to do so, which is abundantly often! So when you see me serving in the community, this is a passion and a spirit that was birthed inside of me from early on. The light that it has allowed me to shine onto others, the spirit of confidence that it has given me, and the positive outlook on life that it has given me, is just a feeling that I often cannot put into words. Serving has always created an avenue for me to shine my light, even if I may be experiencing a dark time. Oftentimes, serving others will help you to get through a dark time.

Benefits of Service

Let's review some of the benefits of service, and how lending a helpful hand to someone, or an organization, can impact your inner light and help improve your health and happiness.

Serving allows you to meet other people

When you are out in the community supporting a cause, or giving back, you are bound to meet someone whom you do not know. Sometimes we don't always understand how fate works, but if you are strategically placed in a particular setting at a particular time, it was supposed to be that way, as Pastor T.D. Jakes states, "Nothing "just" happens". I believe that everything is under divine order and timing. So if you are out assisting in an effort and lending a hand, you will more often than not meet people who are like-minded and have a good spirit. I enjoy being out in the community as I learn so much from other people just by observing, or even starting a conversation. Sometimes you may be standing next to someone who says just the right thing at the right time, which is what you may have needed at that moment to give you the push and the light you need to keep going. You may end up exchanging contact information, and now you have made yourself a new friend in the long run, or at the least, an acquaintance. So don't ever discount the power of opening up your mouth and introducing yourself to someone you don't know. It may very well be a life-changing moment of light and love.

Serving helps to prolong your mind and body

Have you ever heard the saying, "It's hard to please God while angry?" Well, think about it like this: It's also hard to serve your community while angry. Even if you are perhaps having a not so good day, serving others and lending a hand is a true stress relief of the mind and body. You can't help but release positive hormones when you are helping someone in need, serving a meal, "walking peacefully in an injustice protest or rally, cleaning trash off the street, bringing clothes to a shelter, or reading a book to a classroom of children. Whether you realize it or not, you also increase your self-esteem as you are providing a sense of accomplishment for yourself. When your self-esteem is high, you automatically feel good about yourself, which brightens the light that you give off to others around you.

Also, giving back keeps you in shape, especially if you are engaging in walks, marathons, community gardens, building homes or playgrounds, or anything in which you are non-stationary. You can reduce your blood pressure, lose weight, and lower your mortality rate. Prolonging your body and mind just serves to prolong the length of time that you can shine from the inside out, and in turn provide more of an impact to your surrounding communities.

Serving can propel your career

Depending on what career or area of work you are trying to position yourself in, volunteering in a similar role or at a particular facility that you have aspirations to work at may be the action that will land you exactly where you want to be. Not only will you gain experience in a particular field, you will meet extremely important people who will be able to assist you along the way! You may have an opportunity to fine tune skills that you may need in order to excel in a certain position, such as task management or communication, or even working with a team.

When I was in high school, I remember volunteering as a candy striper at a local hospital in my community. Although I knew from a pretty young age that I wanted to be in the field of healthcare, I didn't know what that looked like exactly. So I volunteered on the weekends. I would work in the hospital gift shop sometimes, and even delivered water and certain things to patients' rooms, under supervision. This gave me an opportunity to be in a hospital setting, to observe clinicians, and to just get a feel for how patients are cared for. While in nursing school at Emory University, I chose to complete my clinical rotations at the hospital at which I wanted to eventually get a position, once I graduated from nursing school. This was extremely beneficial as it not only allowed me to practice my nursing skills, but it allowed me to meet the nurses, physicians, and directors of the units, so that I could make a wise decision when choosing where I wanted to begin my career after graduation. Emory University Midtown Hospital was where I was hired after nursing school, and I spent 8 years of my nursing career there. So, when volunteer opportunities become available, don't automatically write it off as busy work; it just might be the thing that will propel you to where you want to be career-wise!

Serving is fulfilling and provides purpose

How many times have you said to yourself, "I wish I had a hobby," or "I don't know what my purpose in life is outside of work?" Well, volunteering is an extremely great way to explore different activities, interests, and passions. You may pick up a craft that you were unaware that you had skill in, such as sewing, making jewelry, or scrapbooking. As with anything, try to understand why you are doing something. Always begin with "why." Why do I want to volunteer? Why did I choose this particular organization to share my time and talents with? What do I hope to gain by serving this organization? Or, you may be trying to determine in what capacity you want to give back, and with what organization. So you begin by determining your likes and dislikes. Do you prefer elders or children? Do you prefer team activities or solo activities? What sort of time do you have to commit? What talents can you share?

Once you begin to answer these extremely important questions, you will be on a path to identifying your purpose, which will pour over into your everyday life. Many people serve organizations that are a match with their personality and their interests. There are so many different things you can do to serve, and so many different arenas and organizations to serve in, but whichever you choose, make sure you have fun, meet someone new, laugh, and let your light glow through the smile on your face!

Shine Check:

List the current organizations that you are associated with, in which you give back to your local, national, or global communities.

What activities or events do you enjoy serving most? Why?

In what ways has serving benefited you in the areas of meeting someone you never would have met, introducing you to a career, propelling your career, or fulfilling your purpose?

If you could organize your own community service project locally, what would you choose to do? Why? What population of people would you impact, and why?

Notes

_____

_____

_____

_____

_____

_____

_____

_____

_____

_____

_____

_____

_____

_____

Notes

Shine Habit 8

Smile Gorgeous

*"Let us always meet each other with a smile,
for the smile is the beginning of love."*
– Mother Teresa

The Best Curve

After having danced for the Atlanta Falcons organization as a cheerleader, for 7 seasons, I thought that I would have a permanent smile carved into my face! I mean, geesh! We would have to always keep a smile on our faces when on the field, or even off the field at community service events, and appearances. As I began to think about why having a smile was so important when dancing and serving the organization, I realized that a smile is worth so much more than we would imagine. Think about it; a smile is attractive and motivating! Who wants to go to a football game where all of the cheerleaders have frowns on their faces, or look as if they have all just lost their best friends? No one, right?! If cheerleaders or dancers are in a role to cheer on the football team, how boring and unmotivational would it be for the team to look over to a group of gloomy-faced and unspirited ladies, for energy to keep them going? Would this be beneficial in assisting the team to win the game? My guess would be, "No."

Most positive people are drawn to positive-spirited individuals with smiles and positive energy. Have you ever noticed that during a football game, even when the team is not winning, the cheerleaders are still smiling, dancing, and rooting for their team? This is for good reason! The smiling and dancing create energy and a positive atmosphere of confidence, not only for the team but also for the fans. It gives the team and the fans a glimmer of hope that the outcome may turn out favorable. What if we carried that same mindset into our everyday personal lives? How different would our day-to-day happenings turn out if we got out of bed every morning with smiles on our faces, despite our circumstances, and despite how we may be feeling on the inside—smiles that indicate strength and determination; smiles that indicate drive and motivation; smiles that could even indicate fear, with a mindset that we are not going to allow the fear to overtake us; and smiles that indicate the happiness to still be alive and in the land of the living. I have often heard people say, "Well, I am not going to fake a smile if I don't feel like smiling." While I can totally understand the concept behind this, we are who and what we train ourselves to think and feel that we are. I am a strong believer that what we put out in the environment holds power. Who we tell ourselves we are, holds power. How we feel about ourselves holds power. Now, it is quite understandable, if a person is grieving or has suffered an insurmountable loss, that they may not have a smile on their face initially, or for a few days perhaps, or not for a decent amount of time. However, the purpose of this shine habit is not to tell you to ALWAYS smile, but to encourage you and make you aware of the benefits of smiling, and how a simple smile can bring about a feeling of peace, and evoke a happiness that will cause that light inside of you, which may have been dimmed for whatever reason, to shine again.

The Many Shades of a Smile

There is a saying that states, "A smile doesn't always mean that you are happy, but it may just mean that you are strong." I love this one! A smile can mean many different things depending on the circumstance or the trigger. However, smiling is most often associated with pleasurable feelings of happiness, strength, warmth, fun, kindness, health, love, and peace. And whether we agree or not, facial expressions can evoke emotions in other people. Have you ever seen someone yawn and then all of a sudden you are yawning as well? What about crying? I am pretty sure that we all have been in the presence of someone who was full of an emotion that caused them to begin to cry, whether at a funeral, or even a wedding, which in turn triggered us to begin to cry as well. Smiling has this same effect. It is quite hard to be in the presence of someone who is smiling and full of life, and not at least curve your mouth up into a smile at least once. Unless you are someone who lacks emotion, such as a sociopath or clinically diagnosed narcissist, I can bet my last dollar that you will be influenced by the mood of someone you are in the presence of, whether positive or negative. So smiling is just another emotional expression that is innate to us.

Personally speaking, smiling has been a hodge-podge of emotions for me. I smile due to happiness, fear, and strength. You may think, "Well, how in the world can someone smile out of fear?" And this is a good thought because, many times, we may not even realize that we are doing this. Just keep reading this shine habit, and you will find your answer. Most recently, my smile has been evoked by strength—a strength that is almost supernatural and surpasses my own understanding at times. Because of some of the ups and downs that I have lived through in my lifetime, and the favor that has been bestowed upon me, I cannot do anything but smile! I smile at the grace my God has given me, I smile at the peace that I hold in my spirit, knowing that there is not anything that I cannot do if I put my mind and soul into it. I smile at what my future holds, and the happiness I feel, the closer I get to His promises. I smile at those who may wish an ill-will toward me, as I am well aware of Who I belong to. I know that how another individual feels about me doesn't make or break me, so I smile. I smile because I am able to bless others who may have lost hope for themselves after encountering challenging situations and circumstances. All of these reasons to smile continue to allow my light to expand across individuals who also wish to have their inner light shine through their own souls.

Smiling brings with it so many benefits! A 2012 issue of the Business Insider noted that smiling gives the brain as much pleasure as roughly 2,000 bars of chocolate, or a feeling as if you have just been given $25,000. That is one hell of a smile, right?! I love comedy shows and funny movies for this reason. I love to laugh! Laughing allows me to feel like I can tackle anything, and handle any situation, even in the face of fear! Think about a time you had to stand in front of a large crowd to give a talk, and you were fearful or shy—what did you do? Did you shrink into a ball and cry? Or did you find a way to plaster a smile on your face, introduce yourself, and maybe even create a little humor? You may have tried opening your presentation with a joke or an ice-breaker to take the edge off. If you have done the latter, your smile was more than likely out of fear, although you used it to your advantage. So although you are a little nervous or afraid, laughing will cause you to relax a bit and, in turn, cause your audience to probably do the same.

Happy Medicine

As with the sun, smiling releases endorphins or feel-good hormones that automatically create a better mood inside of you. Smiling also can serve to reduce pain! So, the next time you burn your finger on a hot skillet, give it a good laugh—maybe it will hurt a little less! It's worth a try! In addition, smiling has also been shown to lower blood pressure, while increasing productivity. When we are in a happy mood, we tend to get more accomplished, right? For those of you that celebrate holidays, think about this: During the holiday season, you pull the strength from somewhere to go into your garages and storage units, and pull-down lights and decorations, regardless if you are in the holiday spirit or not. You muster up the energy to drive to the mall or even open up your laptops to do some holiday gift shopping. The holidays are generally a happy time of year for those who celebrate; thus, we are more likely to get more motivated to get things done out of enjoyment rather than obligation. I personally love the holidays! I always find pleasure in listening to holiday music, helping my mother put up holiday decorations, making our holiday menus, and sharing the kitchen to cook up some of our favorite holiday dishes! One of my personal favorite benefits of smiling, based on research, is the belief that people who smile often live about 7 years longer than those who don't (outside of a fatal accident or something out of our control). This is due to some of the things we already discussed, such as lower blood pressure, increased immune system, and those feel-good hormones—and don't forget that you will look younger and more attractive when you smile! We could all benefit from this, I'm certain!

Now you may say, "Well, is there a time where I shouldn't smile?" And the answer is, "Of course!" Again, this shine habit is not the *end all, be all* for showing off those pearly whites; it's only a resource to assist you in increasing your happiness, to allow that inner light to shine through that beautiful smile! When we are in serious environments or situations, such as interviews, funerals, or emergencies, we are not smiling. As the saying goes, "There is a time and a place under the sun for EVERYTHING." So use your best judgement in determining these situations. But overall, a smile will produce much more favorable results than a frown. If you ever find yourself in a funk, and are letting life's darkest moments weigh you down, just remember the **S.M.I.L.E.** approach.

S.M.I.L.E.

Shine – When you smile, your light has a route to exit your spirit and brighten up the world.

Motivate – When you smile, you motivate yourself and the next person to keep going.

Ignite – When you smile, you ignite a fire inside of you that is contagious and spreads.

Smile Gorgeous

Love – When you smile, you are providing unconditional love to yourself.

Energize – When you smile, you give your body a burst of energy to complete a task.

Always remember that behind every smile, there is a story that may not be understood...so keep shining, and don't forget to SMILE Gorgeous!

Shine Check:

Now that we are aware of how smiling can evoke feelings of happiness, strength, motivation, love, energy, and kindness, and how it can decrease stress, provide health benefits, and promote longevity, let's take a few moments to reflect on a situation in which you were feeling low, and how using the **S.M.I.L.E.** approach turned a potentially negative situation into a positive one.

What was the specific situation?

How did the situation make you feel?

In what ways would using the **S.M.I.L.E.** approach have changed your situation?

Notes

Notes

Shine Habit 9
You Are Enough

"Your value will never expire...
it will only expand when you stop proving your worth."

For any of you that have ever doubted who you are, why you are, and what your value is, it is my sincere desire that this shine habit will be the beginning of a completely different view of yourself from here on out. With television, expanding technology, social media, hot girl summer movements, an increasing male to female ratio in some eastern and southern states, divorces, and a world filled with quick clicks to pretty much whatever you want, whoever you want, whenever you want, it is no surprise that there is an unspoken decline in the self-worth and the self-value of many individuals, both male and female, whom may not have tapped into their purpose. The divorce rate is at an all-time high. On the contrary, there is a huge increase in entrepreneurial initiatives, self-help blogs, healthy lifestyle/fitness ambitions, international travel, and faith awareness journeys in more recent years. These bursts of projects have really been a joy to witness by many driven and talented women and men, and really speaks to the birth of intentional purpose and an increased awareness of value.

While this more recent movement of self-realization is unprecedented, there is still much to be said and learned about value, worth, and purpose across the board for women of all ages, ethnicities, and cultures. Now don't get me wrong; there is much to be offered and said of our men! However, this will be a female-centered shine habit, with a focus on providing insight into everything that makes us women MORE THAN ENOUGH!

The Birth of Worth

At just about every decade of a female's life, we are met with tests that may question our value, our self-worth, and our purpose, based on historical western and certain religious views of what make up the worth of a female. In understanding self-worth, it is reasonable to believe that self-perception has a starting point. Regardless if we are raised in a household with two parents, in a single-parent environment, or a foster care environment, these historical views are still alive and kicking. Over the years, I have heard many times that a female raised in a two-parent household has a higher perception of her value due to a father being in the household. While this may be true in some cases, based on what was taught in the household, and what was encouraged and celebrated, this is unfortunately not the case across the board. This statement is contingent upon the relationship demonstrated between the parents, in front of the child and toward the child, and how a father may have treated the mother in the household. Whether we choose to acknowledge this or not, a female initially gains her perception of her worth and value from her father, or father-figure. If a female child witnessed her father making fun of her mother's weight, belittling that mother for having an opinion, and slapping her mother around, or watched her mother be both the mother as well as the father in the home, as well as witnessing her father with different women in and out of the house, then that female child may begin to think that being of a larger size is looked down upon, or that a woman is not to voice an opinion in the presence of a man, or that it is okay to be a "side-piece" to a man, and that it is okay for a man to put his hands on a woman, or that a woman should be both the male and the female in the household—unfortunately, leaving adult women to second guess the idea of entertaining the thought of even having a husband. A female can very well be raised in a home with both a mother and father, or two parental figures for YEARS, and still have no idea of who she is as a female, or the priceless worth that she holds within herself. Furthermore, a female can be raised in a single-parent (mother or father) household and know her value 150%, dependent upon what was instilled in her by that single mother or single father, and how that female was treated by other members of her family.

As I journeyed through my younger years to my adolescent years, and to my young adult and now adult years, I picked up my value, self-worth, and purpose along the way; some of which was via my mother as I witnessed her strength and how she unconditionally loved my sister and I, despite her personal journey with my father. She depended on God to see her through many situations, and through the silent fight that she held inside of her, I was able to gain strength. At other times, I picked up these defining principles through everyday experiences with motherly family figures, my uncles, sitcoms such as *The Cosby Show*, and through my social and scholastic experiences.

<u>Voices of Value</u>

My mother did an EXCEPTIONAL job of instilling drive, motivation, and courage inside my sister and me. By placing us in the best schools, programs, and extracurriculars (which made financial sense for her pockets), my mother had a goal to ensure that we were raised with a foundation that would sustain us; a foundation that would make us feel like we could accomplish anything. It was my personal life experiences (discussed in prior shine habits) that provided me with the balance of my value and worth. It was the trials and errors of life. It was the feeling at times that perhaps I wasn't good enough, because my father wasn't in the home; or the fact that I witnessed him abuse my mother; or the fact that I didn't win Miss Learning Academy in elementary school despite my efforts; or the fact I was robbed at gunpoint; experienced an abortion; or the fact that I auditioned for the Atlanta Falcons and was cut during the final round on my very first audition; or that I experienced a divorce after only 3 years of marriage, only for my ex-husband to remarry another woman within 3 months of our divorce being final. Any of these scenarios would certainly cause any female to question her worth to some degree.

Nevertheless, the high self-esteem developed at an early age, a "know your why" mindset, hard lessons learned through experience, and miracles, signs, and wonders from a Higher Power, is what expanded my sense of my value, my worth, and my purpose—situations that granted me achievements despite what I had been through. These encounters positively impacted how I interpreted my value, and provided me with a level of confidence like no other. I didn't get it right all the time. I faced many failures and setbacks, but His grace and mercy sustained me, and continues to do so. I didn't allow those unfortunate experiences to define me. I didn't use them as a crutch. I didn't wallow in pity and pain with a "woe is me" attitude. Despite all the reasons I could have done that, I instead used those events as fuel in my gas tank of life, to push and excel me further and further along my journey—and guess what? You, too, can do the same, with all of the "Shine Habits" we have discussed thus far.

More Than Physical

Experience has always been the best teacher for many of us, although there are some things that we would rather not have learned through experience. However, if we continue to live in our genuine truth, recognize who our Creator is, and authentically express ourselves in all arenas, there is no limit to our worth of who we can become and what we can achieve. Now, some of you may agree or disagree, but from my experience, there is some degree of historical conditioning that has sort of constructed our value as a magnet to our bodies. Regardless of whether you agree or disagree, we must understand that we are more than our bodies, our age, or our beauty when it comes to securing a desired position, a desired status, or a desired person. We were not put on earth merely to fulfill sexual desires—that is the biggest lie from the pit of hell. But instead, we were put here to live a life in full support of our Creator's vision for us as His children; to live a life of self-love; to live a life of loving others as ourselves; to live a life where we have no limits of what we can accomplish; and to live a life where we are not so caught up in listening to society that we forget our truth of equality.

Now, there is nothing wrong with wanting to be healthy, to have a banging body, or to be a timeless beauty, aging backwards like Benjamin Button, but we should strive to accomplish these things for our own self-love, and not for the sake of fulfilling the perception of Western culture, or to compete with the next female who may be attaining more attention. We have to remember that a woman who knows her value and her worth competes with no one. A queen does not worry about anyone taking her crown. Her crown is a gift from God, custom made, and will NEVER fit anyone else's head but her own. Always remember this, ladies!

The Proverbial Woman

There are many past and present cultures, religions, male-dominated environments, and some households that still treat women as inferior, with verbal, psychological, and physical abuse. I am not here to debate this; however, as a Christian, I am here to help you understand the many Christian biblical stories that account for the value of a woman. Proverbs 31 spoke of a woman that was esteemed in all her worth. A woman with a business, a family, who is a homemaker, is trustworthy, stays up late, gets up early, is well-dressed, laughs without fear (remember my prior S.M.I.L.E. Gorgeous shine habit...wink wink), and more than anything, a woman who fears the Lord—ladies, our value is endless and PRICELESS! There is no amount of money, or hot girl summers that can pay for our worth. Think about our sacred wombs that bear life, a function that nothing else on this planet can do! We are more than enough! This sort of value is indescribable! God placed so much value on a woman that he granted her the ability to birth life into this world, and nurture and provide for that life. Men, you obviously are equally important, as you hold the seeds of life that are planted inside of our sacred soil, with the woman holding the passageway to life. This doesn't mean that if you are a woman and are incapable of bearing and producing a child, that you are less valuable! You are EXTREMELY worthy! It just means that there is another supernatural assignment for you to physically give birth to. He will reveal that to you, and you must walk in that assignment and own that assignment.

Please trust me when I say that I do not know the Bible from cover to cover, nor am I here to deliver a sermon. I am also not here to debate varying cultural or religious views. But as a Christian, I would be remiss if I did not acknowledge the ultimate foundation of a woman's worth. Christianity elevated womanhood to its highest level. For all of my ladies that are "okay" with mistreatment by a man because he is "taking care" of you, or throwing money at you, or because you "appear" to be the best looking or hottest thing rolling, or because you tolerate mistreatment just for the sake of "having" a man or a husband—I am here to tell you that you are more than that, and you are more than enough. I speak from experience. I was that woman in my marriage. I wanted a marriage, and wanted a life different than what I saw growing up. I wanted a healthy and a whole family. But I quickly realized that my marriage was anything but this. Afraid and embarrassed, I tolerated more than I should have, smiling on the outside but crying on the inside, while silently fighting with prayer and humility.

We have to remember, when we are out of God's divine order, He will humble us and remind us that He is the hottest thing rolling, and we are merely branches on His tree of life. He has a way of getting our attention when we don't know any better, or even if we know better but choose to go outside of His will for us. There are biblical shine habits, specifically the New Testament, which speaks to how men are to treat, honor, and value women—and how women should treat and respect men. But again, for the purposes of this shine habit , the focus is on the value of a woman, and how we as women can truly understand how valuable we really are in the eyes of a man. This sort of God-fearing treatment of a woman by a man can only happen when there is full alignment between man and His creator. Anything outside of that will manifest a relationship that is out of alignment, disruptive, disturbing, and self-seeking.

Successful and Solo?

In today's culture and society, it is evident that there are many women of various races that are accomplished in their own right, making their own coins, esteemed, philanthropists, "good" women, attractive, and sought after by many men. But there is an increasing commonality amongst this group of women as evidenced by the number of many talk show and radio show dialogues. What is this commonality, you may wonder? We are single! I have witnessed this time and time again with successful women in my circle, in other circles, in the media, and around the world. I have had many conversations regarding this hot topic, which leads me to believe that this is quite a popular discussion. The spoken and unspoken question that is most popular regarding this, is WHY?!

Oftentimes, there is this stigma that there must be something "wrong" with women that are single. I am here to let you know that there is NOTHING "wrong." There are a multitude of reasons why this may be the case for some women. It is evident that women around the world, and in general, face this challenge of singleness. I acknowledge this truth. But after numerous questions, from individuals who do not know my story, inquiring about my singleness at this point in my life, I found it fitting to oblige the topic. Transparently, I have been proposed to twice in my life, and married once in my life. I was engaged at 21 years old, right out of college to someone whom I met while I was at Spelman, and he was at Georgia Tech playing football, later going on to play football in the NFL. But I was extremely too young to get married. I had just made the Atlanta Falcons cheerleaders, and had a whole decade of growth experiences ahead of me. My ex-fiancé had a lot of growing up to do during that time as well, as he was just a few years older than I was, and playing in the league. Years later, I was proposed to again, by my ex-husband, which resulted in a 3-year marriage.

So it is not that some women are single just for the sake of being single. Perhaps some women do not desire to be married. Some may have been married before, and are now on a journey of self-discovery before deciding to join themselves with another again. Maybe some women refuse to settle for what they can do on their own. Marriage is not for the weak or faint of heart. It can be a breath of fresh air if done in accordance with its true intentions. Two people must be on the same page, and seeking the same thing from a marriage. Some women remain single so as not to settle for abuse, entertaining other women in their marriage, spousal neglect, or having to "take care of" a man. I personally do desire to re-marry one day as directed by my Higher Power.

Many accomplished women have achieved their accolades on their own right, and seek a partner that will match or exceed what they bring to the table. Now don't get me wrong; there are tons of accomplished women who may decide to be with someone who may not match or exceed what they themselves bring to the table. And guess what?! These women are held to the fire as well by society. These women are often criticized for being with someone outside of their "league," someone beneath them, someone who is a known cheater, or with someone whom they are "sponsoring." I'm sure you all have heard this before in conversations with your friends, co-workers, etc. Some women and men marry for love, some marry for business, and some marry out of fear of loneliness.

Whatever the reason, the fact remains that it is a choice we all make. There is no right or wrong answer. The only thing we all need to understand is that there is indeed an answer. Marriage is a beautiful institution! I am pro marriage and love to see successful marriages, built on the right soil. Sadly, I would tend to make an educated guess and say that women that choose to settle for abuse, neglect, and cheating in marriages have not found their light as of yet. It is my hope that after reading this shine habit, your soul is illuminated so much that you are in a position to know who you are, the value you hold, and that settling does not have to be an option. You are better than that!

Time for Maintenance

I have a question: Would you take your car to McDonald's to get an alignment? Of course not, right?! Why would you not? Because McDonald's is not equipped to align cars! I would make another educated guess and say that you are more than likely going to take your car to the dealership, or the maker of the car, to get an alignment when your car seems off balance. Why? Because they are the maker of the car, and they know how to align your car! In that same light, we should take our souls and spirits to our Creator when we seem off balance. Our Creator knows exactly how to get us back in line. But what do we do instead? We take our souls and spirits to another person, to an addiction, or to something that we think will fulfill our "fix." We long for in our spirits what only the One who created us can fulfill.

Ladies, when we begin to think that it is okay to be mistreated by a man, whether it is emotional, physical, financial, or spiritual, let's reference the biblical verses listed below, which demonstrate the intended great honor of a woman by a man. In respect for varying beliefs, reference foundational values that you hold as truth and close to your hearts.

1 Peter 3:7
"Husbands, in the same way be considerate as you live with your wives, and treat them with respect..."

Colossians 3:19
"Do not be harsh with your wife."

Proverbs 5:20
"Do not be captivated by other women."

Proverbs 31: 28–29
"Call your wife 'blessed' and praise her."

Hebrews 13:4
"Honor your marriage; keep it pure by remaining true to your wife in every way."

Because we do not live in a perfect world, we are entitled to mistakes, both men and women, but how wonderful that He died for a multitude of our sins! We can go to Him in genuine repentance, and He will make us new. Now, it may not erase some of the consequences we will still face as a result of our actions, but we can live whole again, knowing that He will never leave us or forsake us.

Go Slow to Go Fast

Now let's switch gears. Unfortunately, I have witnessed many women's self-worth being attached to how well we shape up against the next woman, who may be more attractive, have more materialistic gains, or attract more men. I also believe that many of us place a high degree of value on how we are viewed by the men in our society, as well as others, including our parents, siblings, friends, and family. Regarding men, there is this unspoken notion of competition among women, due to the male/female ratio in some places. But ladies, I am here to tell you that WE compete for NO ONE! If we are made in His image, then why are we in competition with one another? Why are we placing so much value on getting the attention of a man? Why are we seeking attention via non-value added avenues, as opposed to seeking purpose in value-added behaviors? We have to first place that value in Him, and in ourselves first. We have to get to know who He is, and who we are, and the value and power that we each hold inside of us. We should compete with no one besides ourselves!

Ladies, we hold so much value! We must place that attention on ourselves, and make sure that we are WHOLE women before seeking a man to determine our worth. We make it extremely easy for a man to come into our lives and dictate our worth, because we may be desperate, lonely, afraid, or plain just don't know any better. If we know who we are, why we are, and who we belong to, then it will be easy to redirect our energy, our time, and ourselves away from anyone who is not suitable for our souls, or necessary for our assignments. The only being that has the authority to determine our value and our purpose, is the One who created it. We may take a few falls, but the beauty is that we get right back up, with a lesson and a blessing, in forward motion toward our true value. Life is tough, gorgeous—but so are you!

Coming to the realization of your **VALUE**, follow these tested tactics, and you will begin to understand how priceless you really are.

<u>VALUE Tactics</u>

Stop giving too much too soon

By nature, ladies, we are nurturers. We have an innate instinct to love, protect, and comfort. This can be both a blessing and a curse: a blessing in that we are naturally born to care for the seeds that are birthed from our wombs, oftentimes without any direction or previous knowledge; and a curse in that we often carry this same energy and God-given trait into relationships right out of the gate, without any thought. Let's pretend you are a brand-new real estate agent, and you have a friend of a friend that was referred to you to potentially assist them with purchasing their first home. This person contacts you to set up a time to speak with you about what they are looking for. Because this is their first home buying experience, and you are new to real estate, you are extremely accommodating. You begin offering information to your potential client, and even agree to show them a few houses that may interest them, to get a feel for what they may be interested in.

After about 5 phone conferences, and going out to show 5 different homes, your potential client tells you that they forgot that their aunt is a real estate agent, and decides to go with their aunt for real estate needs as opposed to you. Bummer, right? Being that you are new, you forgot to have this person sign a Buyer Brokerage Agreement, which would have prevented all of your time, efforts, and energy being wasted. So you now have to chalk this experience up to a learning lesson. This is exactly what happens when we press the pedal to the metal without taking precaution, covering ourselves, and understanding the consequences of our actions in relationships. We have to learn to go slow to go fast, and ensure that all of our checks and balances are in place, before we rush out the gate into a relationship.

When we meet new people, sometimes we tend to dive in headfirst, especially if the person is nice, or attractive, you have chemistry with them, or you don't want to miss out on something that you think is what you have been waiting for. We must realize that sometimes when we mix two beings together and call it chemistry, it may have the potential to blow up in our face. So, we have to be careful when we jump right in, as we just might be jumping into a science project. We have to be sure we are mixing the right chemicals together from a faith, family, and finances standpoint, as opposed to a "face" standpoint. Furthermore, we are extremely accommodating, giving of ourselves, of our time, of our resources, and sometimes our bodies. We talk too much, and offer information that allows the other person to know exactly what they need to do to secure us. Ladies, I have two words for you: SLOW DOWN! When you first meet someone, you don't know this person. You may have prayed and spoke in tongues for God to send you your soulmate. But ladies, again, just as God hears our prayers, so does Satan! Many people will talk a good talk, and maybe even walk a good walk for a while. But soon enough, that walk just might turn into a shuffle if you are not careful. As a Christian, I send my Creator before me in all that I do. I pray for discernment, a wisdom that surpasses what my flesh may not see at times, and for any signs that may not be of Him. Take your time in getting to know a person's motives. Don't rearrange your lifestyle to accommodate someone whom you don't know. Don't offer your very intimate resources, or even open up your inner circle. And most importantly, ladies, don't open up your legs! Hard truth! It is a done deal pretty much after that, as you have just given the most sacred part of your body and your spirit to someone whom you don't know, only for them to see something more attractive, or someone whom can offer more resources to them, and they leave you just as quick as they met you.

I hate to step on a few toes with this next statement, but too much too soon is a sign of desperation. Unless someone has asked you to be exclusive with them, don't ever offer your emotions, or tell them they are the only one, even if they are. This is not playing games—this is being smart! Ladies we have to remember that the egg does not swim to the sperm, the sperm swims to the egg. And once the sperm reach the egg, only one will get in after a very long swim. But look at the outcome after all the work is done; a beautiful life is developed and birthed. We should carry this same concept in our dating worlds. Let this sink in for a bit, and you will be on your way to developing and birthing a beautiful relationship with someone who was meant to get through to you.

You don't have to be an open book with someone you just met, or with someone you have known for quite some time for that matter. Sit back and observe. Ask relevant questions to gather the necessary data that you need in order to make a wise and informed decision on where you want the relationship to go, and whether the person is even qualified to go where you are going! Also, close your wallet, ladies! We are not here to buy a relationship. If the person you are getting to know does something nice for you, you can simply return a creative thank you by getting a simple card with something of little monetary value in it, like a Starbucks gift card if you know he or she is a coffee drinker. Now, once you both have made a mutual commitment that is serious and heading in the direction under God's guidance, then you can start to give just a tad bit more in reciprocity—but even then, ladies, be smart, and keep a little bit of mystery about yourself. You will remain interesting and not end up like our naive real estate agent by giving too much too soon.

Focus on your good...not on your not so good

It is so easy at times to get caught up in what we are not the best at, as opposed to what we can do very well. We, as human beings, are always more critical of our own selves than the next person may be of us. That's okay, as this gives us drive, determination, and motivation to be our very best selves. However, because we each are unique and are made for a very special purpose unique only to us, we all have good within us. Whether you have a gift of listening and thinking critically, or you have excellent organizational skills and love to plan events, there is something inside each of us that makes us more than enough to exist in this world. Perhaps you have Tina Turner or Beyoncé legs and can secure bookings as a leg model. Just know that regardless of what you have gone through that may have caused you to doubt your value or your worth, those gifts and abilities will always be within you.

Many times when we focus on the good, we are so busy understanding how we can capitalize off of our good, that we don't have time to even think about the not so good. When we give ourselves those positive affirmations, we are hardwiring how we feel about ourselves, and creating an environment for those things to manifest within us and around us. Focusing on the *good* allows us to recognize the value we do have and bring to this world. So anytime someone tries to point out something about you that may be considered a *not so good*, out of spite, boldly and proudly look them right in the eye and remind them that there is no perfect person, and that each of us are created for a purpose and in His image. Have no fear in making note of your gifts and your good, and remember that all things come together for the good of those that love Him. I can promise you that whoever was bold enough to point out your *not so good* in a negative manner, will think twice moving forward. Try it and see!

Embrace your flaws...they make you perfectly imperfect

Because we tend to live in a time where mistakes are magnified, we put unnecessary pressure on ourselves to achieve perfection. Let me tell you, there is no such thing as perfection. Perfection is the epitome of insanity—seriously! We were not created to be perfect, only purposeful. I once choreographed a dance for a group of 9th and 10th grade ladies, to Kierra Sheard's "Flaws." In this song, Kierra sings about our flaws and how what we perceive as our flaws are not seen as flaws at all by the One who created us. You may ask, "Well, how is it that flaws can make us perfectly imperfect?" The answer lies in the beauty of acknowledging that we are not perfect, and our flaws are what make us unique and beautiful. There are so many variations of flaws. There may be physical flaws, character flaws, and emotional flaws. Physical flaws are really subjective as we constantly are bombarded with images of a certain body type, hair type, eye-color, facial structure, etc. We can easily say to ourselves, "My teeth are not white enough," or "My hair is not as curly" ...but who determines beauty? Honestly! Who determines beauty?! God and us! What we may consider to be a flaw under everyday societal standards, are actually the things that make us beautiful! Freckles, moles, short hair, long hair, dark skin, light skin, full-figures, slim-figures—are all BEAUTIFUL! If we resist the urge to compare ourselves to others, and accept the next person for who they are as a unique individual, then we will begin to move away from judgement and bias of what is beautiful and what is not.

With character flaws such as stealing, lying, or cheating, you may say to yourself, "Well, there is nothing beautiful about those things!" And in the literal sense, you would be absolutely right! However, the beauty in this comes from the understanding that we all have fallen short, and no one is in a position to judge the other. What we can do is share our own faults, struggles, and consequences (much like I am doing in this book), with the hopes of helping the next person to manage, and potentially overcome, destructive behavior. The commonality is that at the end of the day, we all are limited and need each other for accountability and to survive—how beautiful is that!

Emotional flaws are the hardest at times because, often, these flaws take time and a level of vulnerability to expose to others. I don't care how we want to twist it or turn it, or throw it up in the air like it doesn't exist—we all have some level of an emotional flaw. Something in our past, or (for some of us) something that is happening in our present, caused or is causing us not to have full capacity to trust, love, or feel safe. Listen, there is no embarrassment to be had here—none whatsoever. Once we acknowledge this flaw, we open up about it to someone who we do trust, or to someone who is facing a similar situation, and learn from it. When we do this, we open up the beauty of healing and the ability to help someone else. As the saying goes, "You never know what the person next to you is dealing with." So, dare to allow your flaws, whatever they may be, to be of good use to another. Only then will we begin to see just how perfectly imperfect we truly are.

Be brave enough to know you can have whatever you want without settling

Settling is a word that honestly just makes me itch when I think about it. I am not talking about settling for a cheese pizza over pepperoni because you don't eat meat, and veggie was not an option at the birthday party you took your child to. I am not talking about settling for Circle K gas because your needle was in the red, and the Shell station was 5 miles away. Particularly in this shine habit, I am speaking of settling when it comes to the friends that you choose, or the significant other, companion, partner, or husband that you accept in your life. Whether on television, in your close circles, in schools, in the public, or even in the workplace, some young ladies and women seem to be under the impression that we have to be surrounded by many people to have it going on. Or perhaps the more friends we have, the better off we are, because we are seen as the "it" thing. In addition, I have witnessed ladies settling for having a piece of a man, as opposed to a whole man. I want you to know that to protect your value and your peace when it comes to both friends and significant others, you DO NOT have to settle. Period!

When choosing your circle of friends, remember the earlier shine habit, where we discussed that positive tribes should bring about positive vibes within you, and vice-versa. This is extremely important. Don't settle to have someone around you just for the sake of having someone around you. Any person that you are considering a friend should bring some type of value to your life, and you to theirs. Even if it is because they make your soul happy by giving you a good laugh. Having people in your circle just for popularity decreases your value whether you realize it or not. Think about a queen in her most esteemed and royal position. How many people do you see around her? Seriously?! Maybe 3 people—and these people are her court! They are not *randoms*. They were chosen for a purpose, as a queen's court brings value to her, and she to them. A queen's court is able to support her in the event she is not able to fulfill a duty. This is what a friend is supposed to be able to do for you—be there to support you, fill in for you, assist you in becoming your best self, and to be alongside you in the event you cannot fulfill something in your life. This creates a high-value friendship, one in which both people are growing and learning from each other.

Don't settle to have people around you because they make you "look" good, or you are, or they are, riding off of a status that either may bring to the table. Having someone around you of status, who is not pouring into you, or encompassing a mutual exchange of knowledge or resources, is not of value. I can recall someone close to me always feeling it necessary to "name drop" on any given occasion. This person knew, and had quite a few "well-known" individuals, or celebrities as friends. This person would always want to be in the presence of their well-known friends, but on one occasion desperately needed help as they had gotten into a situation. When this person began speaking of the people in their circle whom they were considering reaching out to, they noted that they could not reach out to the "well-known" individuals as those people would "cut" them off. I thought to myself, "Very interesting. How is it that you are considering these so-called "well-known" individuals' close friends of yours, you talk to them all the time, but you can't open up to them in a serious situation where you are in need because they will "cut" you off?!" What is going on here? In any relationship, there should be balance. This a classic description of someone who is seeking external validation to make themselves feel good about themselves, but silently do not have anyone to turn too in true times of need. So I encourage you to examine your circle. Ask yourself these very important questions, and see if you have a high-value court or not.

- Who is in your court?
- What is the true relationship?
- Are they able to fill in for you in the event you are not able to fill in for yourself?
* What are you learning from your circle?
- What are you bringing to your circle in terms of what they could learn from you?

When it comes to significant others—companions, boyfriends, baes, fiancés, or husbands—the same holds true. Sometimes we allow other people's lives, relationships, marriages, social media timelines, biological clocks, age, self-esteem issues, etc. to dictate who we decide to join ourselves with. I have one word for this: DON'T! You do not have to let go of the things that are important to who you are, what you believe in, or how you would like to be treated and loved. Although we are all on a journey to the finish line of life, settling will not help you along the way—trust me. It may only hinder you. And I do speak from experience, as I once settled for someone that was a nicely wrapped package with a big shiny bow, who seemed to have all the bells and whistles. But when I was finally able to unwrap that nicely wrapped package, pull off the bow, move all the tissue paper out of the way, and dig into the box, I found out that there was really nothing in the box that was of use to me or my future. And that was when the disappointment set in, because in my mind, it was too late. But I could not blame anyone but myself. I had to be accountable. I had not taken the time to unwrap the big shiny box when I first received it. I wanted the box to stay wrapped because it was so well put together. On the outside, it seemed like the perfect gift; but on the inside, it was hollow. Out of denial and confusion, I wanted to continue to think that I had this nice shiny gift, but that didn't work either. I don't care how much I tried to flip the box upside down and turn it to the side, it was still the same hollow box.

Think about the holiday season for those that celebrate the holidays. You attend a white elephant gift exchange. All the gifts are laid out in front of you, and you are excited to choose your gift as it is finally your turn! You look around and choose the biggest, most beautifully wrapped gift! You don't even open it right away because you want to wait until you get home—you don't want anyone to see your gift, as they may try to steal it. Once you get home, you unwrap your beautifully wrapped gift, only to find that it is a box of popcorn, and you don't even like popcorn! Poor you! If only you had unwrapped it at the party, you would have had a chance to potentially choose another gift. But because you didn't, you are now stuck with this box of popcorn that you don't even like. This is exactly what happens when we settle in relationships with significant others. We are so excited about a person's physical attributes, their status, what type of vehicle they drive, and what type of job they have, that we fail to try to understand what type of heart they have, or if they even have a heart for people, or if they want the same things in life that we do. And if they have a faith, what is that faith? And many more things that we fail to try to understand.

Once we begin to grow in our maturity, or we go through a few mishaps in relationships, or we start to gain knowledge, we begin to re-evaluate the way we have been going about who we choose to have in our lives. Whether you agree or disagree, just know that our God did not put us in this earthly realm to settle. His plans were for good and not for evil; his plans were to give us a future and a hope (Jeremiah 29:11). Where is the future in settling? The future in settling is a life of bitterness and upset. I'm sure that is not what you want. The good thing is that it is never too late to change your situation for the better, or to begin to take measures to ensure you are not settling, even if you are already married. I am not asking you to run out and get a divorce, as I am pro-marriage if it is of God, and was brought together by God. If you are already married, and you have unhappily settled, just know that all is not lost for you. If you are of faith, pray and petition your Higher Power to lead you in your thoughts, your actions, and next steps of His will for you. If you are married and happily settled, then best wishes and continued peace and happiness to you in your settlement. God can be in the midst of settled marriages if they are brought under His direction. He can and will bless them.

In healthy relationships, you will never feel as if you are compromising your value or your worth. No one is perfect, so there may be some expectations that are not met, but these things will not be deal breakers. If they are deal breakers, and you find yourself continuing the relationship, you just might be settling, and I would hate for you to find yourself in that situation.

To help ensure that you are not settling, here are a list of **VALUE tactics** that you can do to start receiving what you want, to create a life of value and happiness.

1. Heal any prior wounds.
2. Practice self-love.
3. Set stricter boundaries.
4. Stop making excuses.
5. Stop bending over backwards.
6. Expect quality communication.
7. Make sure words and actions align.
8. Make a list of the qualities of the person.
9. Expect more.
10. Understand your non-negotiables.
11. Don't stop your hobbies and interests.
12. Discuss what hurts you and what makes you happy.
13. Don't try to change a person, just move on if not in alignment with what you seek.
14. Know that being single is not a curse.

Once you understand your value and your worth, you will no longer be on the clearance rack, but instead under the counter in a velvet drawer! Thank me later!

Shine Check:

Are you currently in a relationship in which you are not exercising the **VALUE tactics**? What reasons do you believe you are jeopardizing your value for the relationship? What fears do you have?

Once you have recognized your reasons for jeopardizing your value and your worth for a given relationship, in what specific ways can you begin to exercise the **VALUE tactics** to increase your worth?

If you feel that you are in a violent relationship, where physical abuse is occurring, please know that you don't have to be, and there is help for you. If in immediate danger, please call 911. For 24/7, confidential help, please call the National Domestic Violence Hotline, at 1-800-799-7233.

Notes

Notes

Shine Habit 10
L.I.T. (Live Intentionally Today)

"In the end, we only regret the chances we didn't take."

Contrary to the unfavorable description of being intoxicated, there is a slang term that is frequently used currently by Generation Y and the Millennials, to describe something that is "exciting," "excellent," or "extremely great." It's called being L.I.T.! Now, whether you have heard of this term or not, we can all agree that a state of extreme excitement can be considered favorable and positive. For the purposes of this book, and regardless of known meanings, L.I.T. (Live Intentionally Today) will translate to living a life of intention, today and every day—walking in a light so bright that you cannot help but be LIT!

Low Light

Day in and day out, I see our women, men, and children walking with an unfavorable low light or no light around them at all! And perhaps this is due to circumstances that have impacted who they were truly meant to manifest into. "How do you know, you may ask?" My heartfelt answer is that I know because of the negative conversations I hear, the facial expressions I see, the unspoken body language that so many of us display, and the self-sabotaging choices that we all may have made along the way.

Sadly, many of these circumstances may have been out of the control of the afflicted individual; circumstances that many times have roots in our childhood experiences, which expanded into young adulthood, middle age years, and our final years. Contrary to any unfavorable circumstance any of us may have endured, I highly believe that each of us serve a greater purpose in this earthly realm. So, this journey of life and love that we all are on is to discover our purpose through an array of ups, downs, twists-and-turns, tears, smiles, victories, and defeats—all while serving a power higher than ourselves to guide us along the uneven roads of life. We were not meant to operate under low light, under low vibrations, or in darkness. Our objective is to live a life full of abundance—so much so, we can't contain it all—and by default are induced to share our overflow with our neighbors, so that our neighbors will gain the strength and the courage to have the same untiring faith in serving a power greater than themselves, to receive a life of abundance.

<u>Greater than Yourself</u>

"Serving a power higher than ourselves, and being spiritual, may mean quite a few different things to many different people. It is a broad concept, encompassing many different perspectives. Spirituality can mean being connected to a source of positive light, having faith in a power higher than yourself, loving your neighbor as yourself, and walking in a light that is reflective of your Higher Power as your ultimate purpose." Henceforth, I state my following statement with sensitivity: "I believe that having faith and being spiritual does not exempt us from making mistakes or witnessing calamities." I am a walking witness to this, as you have had the opportunity to explore along this journey. The journey we have gone on together in this book of light and love has hopefully made it clear that no one is perfect. We all have fallen short, and will fall short in our futures. But faith is the incentive to get back up and begin again, with a knowledge that your promise will manifest, and with an incentive to work to create a L.I.T. life—a life full of the most remarkable and greatest intentions.

I believe that "all things work together for the good of a Higher Power and purpose." Although life can sometimes serve us a plate of hard-knock situations, this doesn't mean that we no longer have purpose. Our purpose is still inside us! We just have to begin to understand how the light we give off can either help us or hinder us from reaching our purpose. Better yet, whatever your hard-knocks are, they may very well be the drive that you need to push a little harder, and go the extra mile every day to live with intention.

In order to live a L.I.T. life, and shine from the inside out, we learned we must love ourselves FIRST in order to love others. In order to love yourself first, you must understand whom you belong to and why. The fact that I now love myself wholly, allowed me to display love to you through this book. If I had not yet taken the time to invest in myself and refill my own cup, I would not have been in any shape to pour into you. Trust me, I had to get to the point where I fully loved myself. It wasn't always this way or this easy, as you have witnessed. I am in my 3rd decade of life, and I am finally at a point where I can say that I truly love myself! I love myself with EVERYTHING I have, because I now recognize who

I am. I recognize my value in a world where value is not given much attention anymore. Through all of my dark shadows, I kept my eyes on my Light, my Love, and my Lord, which has allowed me to continue to shine despite some really dark times—and now, I live a truly L.I.T. life.

Be Intentional

Given the hand of unfavorable experiences that I was dealt and, in some instances, allowed to be dealt, I would have never guessed that I would now be sitting and sharing with all of you, about how I turned my many dark shadows into high vibrations of light and love. And I do have a plethora of recorded bright moments from my past, which have equipped me with skills to lead a L.I.T. life. It is my most sincere hope that these moments will be equally as inspiring to you as you walk along your L.I.T. path. Some of these humble accolades achieved while along my journey were: graduating Valedictorian of my elementary school; being crowned Prom Queen and Miss Black Teen of Atlanta, all in the same year of 1998; graduating Spelman College cum laude; winning Miss Photogenic in the 2007 Miss GA USA pageant; serving as captain for the Atlanta Falcon Cheerleaders, where I traveled to five international countries to perform for American troops stationed in these countries; being featured in a 2002 issue of *Ebony* magazine, in an article highlighting African-American NFL cheerleaders; being featured in the *Atlanta Journal-Constitution's Pulse Magazine,* in the article, "From Scrubs to Pom-Poms," as a registered nurse who had pom-poms in her back pocket and a stethoscope in her hand; being the youngest to be inducted into Chamblee High School's inaugural Hall of

Fame; becoming a professional Samba dancer after a trip to Brazil on a whim; modeling for a top Atlanta agency and participating in some of the most memorable events of my life; serving my beloved Alpha Kappa Alpha Sorority, Inc., in which I have mentored young girls and ladies in becoming a better version of themselves; earning a Master's in Nursing Leadership degree, and sitting with CEOs, CMOs, and VPs to understand better ways to increase the quality of health for patients, all while reducing cost and providing an exceptional patient experience; and writing my first book as a precursor to the launch of my independent small business and nonprofit organization.

Now you may think to yourself, "How were you able to accomplish all these bright moments, despite your dark moments?" And the answer is simple: I have a loving mother who instilled drive in me, and I was discrete in my goals from early on, and INTENTIONAL in everything I set my eyes on! I also understood who I belonged to, at an early age, after having many encounters with Him. Once I understood this very important concept, everything else followed.

Now granted, we are faced with choices we have to make in life, and as you have witnessed, I didn't always make the best choices, as we have explored. It was when I depended on myself, and leaned unto my own understanding, that I typically made poor choices. There were always consequences, but He never left me. At other times, I leaned on what my mother taught me growing up, even before I could comprehend what having a faith even meant. She taught me to love my neighbor as myself, to be aware of certain uncomplimentary crowds, to not use foul language, to take care of my body, to always ask questions if I don't understand something, etc. The one thing I found when I was able to comprehend having faith, and when my mom bought me my first Bible, was that much of what she taught me was already written in the good book! And although I knew better in some instances, I didn't always do better, as we have explored.

<u>Never Lose, Only Learn</u>

We can never fail when we are living a L.I.T. life. We can only learn, but never lose. Each of you are exceptional in all of your ways. That fire that has always been deep inside you now has the oxygen it needs to blaze brighter than it ever has. A fire that will allow you to accomplish dreams and desires that you have always had your heart set on. A fire that will now allow you to forgive those who may have wronged you in some manner, and prevented you from living intentionally because of a burden of non-forgiveness that you wore over your head.

To live a L.I.T. life doesn't mean that we will live a perfect life, but it does mean we will live a life of intention based on those life strategies, behaviors, and shine habits that we know to be true. A life of aim and purpose. A life where we are determined to make a positive difference in the lives of people we meet—a legacy living life.

After all, you have just taken a journey along the road of shining from the inside out. Along the way, it is my sincere prayer that you have truly captured the essence of various habits that have worked for me, which may very well work for you in becoming a beacon of light that radiates in the darkest of places, times, situations, and people—keeping you living a life of intention and light, day in and day out!

Shine Check:

If you do not feel that you are living a L.I.T. life, what are some behaviors you could adopt to begin living a life of intention? Create a daily schedule of activities that will positively contribute to you living a life of intention every day, beginning from when you get out of bed, to when you return to bed. If you find that your daily schedule consists of activities that are not positively contributing to your purpose, re-evaluate your activities. This is a great opportunity to consider other activities that will align with your purpose, and ensure you are living intentionally every day.

Notes

_____

_____

_____

_____

_____

_____

_____

_____

_____

_____

_____

_____

_____

Notes

AFTERWORD

Congratulations! You did it! We started this journey of light and love with **knowing our why**, and understanding our purpose. That purpose is rooted in our Higher Power. A purpose to leave a legacy rooted in service. A legacy of service that is often realized through pain, whether personal pain or witnessed pain. As we continued along our journey, we stopped at a rest area of **self-love**, which taught us to create a love sparkle within ourselves, to invest energy and positivity into our inner spirits first. Only when we are filled with self-love are we able to continue our individual journeys of spreading love to others. We came to understand what it means to **be uniquely you**, and embrace our differences for all they're worth. It is so easy to fall in line with others around us, or strive to be consistent with the hype of our generation. But it is when we hold true to our individual thumbprints that only we encompass, that we truly light up our environment. Even if our environment is filled with individuals that wish us ill will, or does not have our best interest at heart, we learned that **kindness is truly the ultimate killer**. Unexpected kindness is the most powerful, least costly, and most underrated agent of human change.

Furthermore, we begin to realize how to display **positive vibes to attract positive tribes**. A good rule of thumb is to ask yourself this question: "If I was on the outside looking in, would I want to be around me?" If your answer to this question is anything other than yes, then you, my dear, have a little bit of work to do, and I suggest re-reading Shine Habit 5. Better yet, if you are finding it difficult to pull yourself out of a negative space, it may serve you well to load up on a dose of **Vitamin N (Nature)**, or get out in your community and **serve honey**! When you are treating your spirit to a healthy dose of the sun, fresh air, healthy fruits and vegetables, or serving in your local communities, it will be hard to have anything other than that of a positive attitude.

Life will sometimes get the best of us and cause a shadow to come over our spirits, but even in those dark times, always remember to **smile gorgeous,** and **know you are enough**. As the good book states, "trouble doesn't last always," and your smile will be a reminder to yourself of this fact.

Lastly, when living a **L.I.T.** life, we understand our why, our purpose, our value, and our worth, on a level that ignores and redirects any and everything that tries to come against that; and without hesitation, we can live a life full of intention every day. A life that truly allows our inner light to continuously shine because our spirit is whole and healed. A life in which we strive to have our daily activities line up with our purpose. A life that is in harmony with the newfound fire burning inside of us—giving off a glow so bright that it is blinding to those who still walk in shadows. With the inner light that you will now give off, I have full confidence that you will be able to light a path for those in the dark, to guide them along their journey to sunshine.

Once you begin to apply the **10 Shine Habits** that you have learned along this journey, you will begin to realize how your life will begin to transform right before your own eyes. The more your

Afterword

life transforms in the most positive way, your desire and drive for success will continue to increase, causing you to seek out opportunities to reach back and share with generations behind you, the very habits that brought you from darkness into the light. Living a L.I.T. life is the only way to go, and once you go L.I.T., it is my prayer that you will not quit!

~~Love Brencia

ACKNOWLEDGEMENTS

I would like to give all thanks and honor to my Lord and Savior, Jesus Christ, for instilling in me the will, the drive, the faith, the vulnerability, and the determination to write a piece that not only exposes my dark moments, but provides a foundation for all to shine in the most magnificent way. Thank you for living in me, and never leaving my side Daddy.

Secondly, I thank my mother, Otheree Bienville, and my sister, Bridgette Bienville, for believing in me when I initially said that I wanted to write a book, back in the summer of 2018.Your encouragement and your support is unmatched. I love you, and I thank you from the bottom of my heart.

Next, I would like to thank my publishing company, the Aaron Raymond Group, for providing an avenue for me to write my first book. The 10-10-10 program was a great tool to guide me and ensure that my book would be a WOW factor! My book architects, Liz Ventrella and Christina Fife, were there every step of the way to answer my questions and ensure I was on track. Thank you! To my editor Lisa Browning, and book cover lead designer, Waqas Ahmed, I sincerely thank you both. To RaQuita Weathers of Belle Rouge Photography, the cover shot was AMAZING! Thank you!

To my cousin and author of *Just Get Up: And Manifest Your Inner Genius*, Isaac Miller, I sincerely have no words. You are the best. Thank you for the advice, the late-night calls, emails, text messages, and mentorship to ensure that my piece was exceptional! You are unmatched.

Lastly, to all of my family, friends, followers, sorority sisters, and anyone who encouraged me and cheered me on along the way, THANK YOU! Your love and enthusiasm was heartfelt, and I love you all!

ABOUT THE AUTHOR

Brencia K. Bienville grew up bright-eyed and full of life in a single-parent household, in New Orleans, LA, with her mother, Otheree Bienville, and her older sister, Bridgette Bienville. Although she witnessed extreme domestic violence and many gut-wrenching dark trials at an early age, coupled with an unforeseen divorce after 3 years of an up and down abusive marriage, her life experiences have allowed her to navigate a life painted with a mixture of dark and light experiences. Her dark experiences and valuable lessons learned allowed her to write her first book, *The Light of My Shadows: 10 Habits to Shine from the Inside Out*. She is humbled and thankful to her Lord above for the grace and mercy bestowed to allow her to be a Registered Professional Nurse, former 7-year Atlanta Falcons cheerleader and captain, print model, professional and principal samba dancer for Fogo Brasil Arts and Entertainment, choreographer, and author.

Brencia has a passion for various cultures, foods, and people, and has traveled to many countries, including Brazil, Canada, Mexico, Puerto Rico, Cuba, Bahamas, Jamaica, Tokyo, Portugal, Greece, Italy, and Egypt—the last five of which she had the humbling opportunity, in 2008, to perform for U.S. soldiers stationed there. She was featured in the *Atlanta Journal Constitution's Pulse Magazine*, in an article titled "From Scrubs to Pom-Poms," in 2006, and has made numerous appearances on local and non-local news stations and television shows across her nursing and dance careers.

Brencia is an active member of Alpha Kappa Alpha Sorority, Inc., and faithfully extends her time and talents to her local community. She believes that serving others is a very important habit in shining your light from the inside out. Brencia currently resides in Atlanta, GA., where she is diligently working on the launch of her upcoming small business and non-profit organization under her company name, Light of My Shadows, L.L.C. She enjoys fitness, dance, cooking, travel and outdoor activities.